SCREEN DECO

Ann Sothern in *Let's Fall in Love* (1934).

SCREEN DECO

Howard Mandelbaum

Eric Myers

COLUMBUS
BOOKS

791·43

Dedicated to:
Metro-Goldwyn-Mayer, Paramount,
Warner Brothers, Twentieth Century-Fox, R.K.O.,
Universal, Columbia, and United Artists

Test shot from MGM's *Hollywood Party* (1934).

Contents

Frank Morgan in *Paradise for Three* (1938).

Acknowledgments

The authors wish to thank Phototeque for its generosity in providing most of the visual material in this book. Our gratitude also to Elliott Stein, Lawrence O'Toole, Kenneth Anger, and David Chierichetti for their time and erudition.

Charles Silver, Cathy Surowiec, and Ron Magliosi of the Museum of Modern Art Study Center gave us their time and the following gave us their stills: Elliott Stein, William Kenly, Marc Wanamaker of Bison Archive, and Ronald Mandelbaum. Additional stills are from Mary Corliss of the Museum of Modern Art, Elisabeth Coppens of the Cinémathèque Royale in Belgium, Jerry Ohlinger's Movie Material Store, Ken Hollywood, Bob Colman, Eddie Brandt's Saturday Matinee, Collector's Book Store, and Cinemabilia.

Thanks to the staff at St. Martin's Press, especially design director Manny Paul and our editor Brian DeFiore, who cheerfully fueled us with support and sushi.

For their generous assistance: Annette Insdorf, Steve Soba, Stephen Harvey, Michael Webb, Mark Mancini, Bill Rippner, H. Pierre Montiel, Howard Feinstein, Marvin Bevans, Jim and Liz Trupin, Larry Sutter, Robert Hofler, George Jenkins, Michael O'Donoghue, Barry Secunda, Penny Stallings, and William K. Everson.

Special thanks to Nicholas Sapieh of Art Resources. Howard Mandelbaum expresses warmest thanks to Mark Colson. Eric Myers wishes to give fond thanks to Mary Guggenheim, Samson De Brier, Ed Margulies, and Jerome Wile, all of whom extended early encouragement.

SCREEN DECO

364·20

This Modern Age

INTRODUCTION

Art and technology began to fuse during the 1920s. The five years of the Great War, with its tanks, airplanes, and submarines; the birth of the skyscraper; the widespread use of electricity—these were creating a second Industrial Revolution. An awareness was taking hold—of power, energy, and speed. More than ever before, the emphasis in daily life was on the "modern" and the futuristic. The result was a style that exploded with wit, elegance, and verve.

Known then as Modernism and now as Art Deco, it was a style so rooted in change that its life span could not possibly be long nor its elements consistent. The term *Art Deco* encompasses everything from the ornate zigzags of the movement's infancy in the early twenties through the stripped-down, streamlined geometric forms of thirties Moderne. Art Deco was closely allied to the fantasies of wealth and elegance prevalent in America between the wars. Naturally, it was right at home in Hollywood.

Movie executives—many of whom were from the fashion trade and understood marketing design—embraced this new style. Former glove salesman Sam Goldwyn and former furrier Adolph Zukor could see that Art Deco's clean lines gave their stars greater freedom of movement. Furthermore, as men who had risen to power in a relatively short time, they perceived Deco as an upscale emblem—ideal as a scenic shorthand for establishing milieu, attitudes, and aspirations. As art director Léon Barsacq wrote in 1970, "A set must take into account the psychology and behavior of those intended to inhabit it."

Joan Crawford in *Our Dancing Daughters* (1928).

A Question of Terminology

Although Art Deco was in the forefront of popular design, the precepts of the Bauhaus and the International Style were also beginning to make themselves felt throughout Europe and America. And by 1932 American designer Norman Bel Geddes had introduced the concept of streamlining in his book *Horizons*. These influences began to effect a change away from the ziggurats of late twenties Deco toward a broader, more spacious type of design. Still highly geometric, this style leaned toward more spartan curvilinear forms with white as the dominant color, distinguished by a marked reduction in ornamentation and by the use of the streamline as the major decorative accent. Streamline Moderne became the leading design style of the thirties, exemplified in such creations as the New York World's

Ginger Rogers in *Shall We Dance* (1937).

Production shot from Universal's *Broadway* (1929), including the crane which was specially constructed to encompass this immense set.

The "Straw Hat" number from *Folies Bergere* (1935), featuring Maurice Chevalier and Ann Sothern.

Fair and virtually the entire Astaire-Rogers series. But this gives rise to confusion: if the Astaire-Rogers films are Streamline Moderne, why are they also called classic Art Deco?

The problem is due to the inadequacy of the term *Art Deco*, which has been used for nearly the past twenty years as a sort of catchall. It was coined in 1966, at the time of a Musée des Arts Décoratifs retrospective of the 1925 Paris Exposition, and has been bandied about ever since as an easy description of any and every style that emerged between the wars. Nineteen-twenties Modernism, Streamline Moderne, International Style, Bauhaus, Russian Constructivism—all have been labeled "Art Deco" by the layman, only causing complications as we attempt to gain a reasoned perspective on the kaleidoscopic design concepts of that very rich era. To facilitate matters, art historians are now tending to use *Art Deco* strictly to describe the Modernistic style that emerged from the 1925 Paris Exposition and flourished until the very early thirties. *Streamline Moderne* (or *Art Moderne*) is used to describe Deco's mid- and late-thirties transformation. The text of this book attempts to adhere to these admittedly generalized guidelines, but the book's concept—and its title—find a parallel in a quote from Richard Guy Wilson in volume 3, number 3, of *Art Deco Society of New York News:*

> If we can use the term Art Deco not to designate a specific style, but rather in the sense that it is inclusive and connotes the tremendous fertility of ideas, culture and design, beginning in the early 20th century and reaching a peak in the 1920's and 1930's, we will better serve our purpose.

Art Deco on Film

Not surprisingly, the first use of Art Deco in film was in France. Director Marcel l'Herbier, always sensitive to new currents in design, hired some of the most adventurous artists in the country to conceive the decor for his films. Elements of the new decorative art began appearing as early as his 1919 *Le Carnaval des vérités,* designed by Michel Dufet and Claude Autant-Lara. L'Herbier's most audacious experiment, however, was *L'Inhumaine* (1923). This cruel, fantastic love story took place in an atmosphere of ultramodern decadence which L'Herbier emphasized by hiring four great designing talents: art directors Alberto Cavalcanti and Autant-Lara, artist Fernand Léger, and architect Robert Mallet-Stevens. To a French moviegoing public weaned on such traditional styles as Empire and Louis XV, the effect was shocking. (The Exposition des Arts Décoratifs et Industriels Modernes was still two years away.) But the film was rightfully admired by many as a brilliant showcase of contemporary French design and as a sumptuous and satisfying thriller. L'Herbier courageously continued to use modern designers for his subsequent films of the

Scene from Marcel L'Herbier's *L'Inhumaine* (France, 1923). Robert Mallet-Stevens in front of the house he designed, with Jacques Catelain and L'Herbier.

6

Laboratory designed by Fernand Léger.

twenties and thirties, including *Le Vertige, Feu Mathias Pascal, L'Argent* and *Le Parfum de la dame en noir.*

The American film industry, though slow to warm to Art Deco, made a few notable experiments in the early twenties which showed an awareness of European design trends. Joseph Urban is credited as the first art director to utilize modern decor in the 1921 William Randolph Hearst production *Enchantment,* starring Marion Davies. Urban followed this with *The Young Diana* (1922), which also boasted astonishingly modern sets. Urban's Wiener Werkstätte background was very much in

Joseph Urban's sets for *Enchantment* (1921) are acknowledged as the first use of modern design in the American cinema.

Natacha Rambova showed an early awareness of trends in French decorative art when she designed the American production *Camille* (1921), with Alla Nazimova and Rudolph Valentino.

Greta Garbo, director Jacques Feyder, and cameraman William Daniels during the filming of *The Kiss* (1929).

Pauline Starke in *Women Love Diamonds* (1927).

evidence in these films. In 1921 Natacha Rambova designed a *Camille* which starred her husband Rudolph Valentino and Alla Nazimova. Rambova's style, a mixture of Art Nouveau and early French Deco, lent a dreamlike quality to the film. Rambova also designed Nazimova's *Salome* (1922), based largely on the Art Nouveau engravings of Aubrey Beardsley. Unfortunately, Rambova turned away from designing in order to manage her husband's career, a move that did Valentino more harm than good and certainly deprived the screen of one of its most adventurous and promising art directors.

Cedric Gibbons may have been the only Hollywood designer to attend the 1925 Exposition in Paris. That visit had a profound impact on him, shaping his style for the next twenty years. Gibbons imposed an all-Deco scheme on the Joan Crawford vehicle *Our Dancing Daughters* (1928), the first American movie to fully exploit the new Modernist decor. The film took the country by storm, garnering particular attention for its striking sets.

The movie that started it all: MGM's *Our Dancing Daughters* (1928), starring Joan Crawford, Anita Page, and Johnny Mack Brown, with sets credited to Cedric Gibbons.

Anita Page in *Our Dancing Daughters.*

Other studios immediately began to put Art Deco sets into their films. Paramount's *The Magnificent Flirt* (1928), designed by Van Nest Polglase, boasted in its publicity that it was making full use of "the new French Decorative Art." Deco sets had enormous drawing power, and even the smaller studios incorporated them into their product. A suggested catchline from the pressbook of Columbia's *Ladies Must Live* (1930) read: "Smart society, gorgeous gowns, polo games, the beach at Newport, modernistic settings—all seen in *Ladies Must Live*, scintillating comedy-drama."

If movies promised life, liberty, and the pursuit of riches, then Art Deco provided the perfect setting. Although characters were often permitted to live better than their incomes would normally allow, decor had to suit the situation. Obviously, films depicting the home life of a stuffy millionaire or struggling clerk could not present the latest in Deco design. Most closely associated with Art Deco were the nouveau riche, the underworld, the worlds of entertainment, travel, and retailing, and women either kept or liberated.

Since movies generally encompassed a number of settings, few films were all-Deco. Deco and more conventional styles co-existed and contrasted in a film the same way a mistress and wife would, each with its place in the overall scheme. For instance, in *The Divorcee* (1930), the New York apartment of Norma Shearer and her newspaperman husband Chester Morris is decorated in tasteful late-twenties style with some Deco touches such as chevron-shaped wall sconces, geometric paintings, and Deco coffee cups and dishes in the kitchen. But when the couple go night-clubbing with their richer friends, the milieu goes spectacularly Deco, and when Shearer strays, adultery is committed in Robert Montgomery's sinfully modern bachelor apartment.

Similarly, in *Wonder of Women* (1929), Lewis Stone shares a tranquil house by the sea with his brunette wife Peggy Wood when not visiting the jazzy digs of blonde Leila Hyams. One setting represents spiritual love; the other lust. The association between Deco and decadence is clear.

Hollywood helped propagate Art Deco. Not only did movies reach millions of people, but the lush lifestyles of movie stars served as inspiration for magazine readers everywhere. Rich clients of Cedric Gibbons would ask for exact duplications of settings he had created for the screen. Gibbons also received requests from newlyweds and engaged couples for blueprints of the dream houses seen at their local Bijou. Stars themselves tried to recreate soundstage magic. For some, there was only a thin line between the sets in which they acted during the day and the homes to which they returned at night. Ginger Rogers's thirties house was designed by Van Nest Polglase and his RKO art department, while Ramon Navarro's plush Lloyd Wright house was decorated by Gibbons all in black fur and silver. For the sake of aesthetic consistency, dinner guests were commanded by Navarro to wear black, white, and silver only.

1133-2/3

Norma Shearer on the town in *The Divorcee* (1930).

"The 20th Amendment," a 1930 short subject dealing with "ultra-modern life in 1950."

(*Left*) *The Magnificent Flirt* (1928).

The love nest of Lewis Stone and Leila Hyams in *Wonder of Women* (1929).

Though the Deco era is recalled for its dizzy abandon, there were opposing currents of conservatism. The appeal of Art Deco in the American home was really limited to the smart set. The middle classes tended to prefer cozy period styles modeled on English cottages or New England farmhouses, while old money clung to more traditional modes such as Tudor, Spanish Revival, Colonial, or Beaux Arts. Those accustomed to wainscoting and Oriental carpeting shunned such twentieth-century industrial materials as glass brick, Vitaglass, Vitriolite, and Bakelite, and found Deco lines harsh and vulgar. That hearty Victorian Ethel Barrymore dismissed the twenties as "a period of ugliness, of ugly fashions, ugly manners, even ugly dances like the Charleston." Similarly, French art director Léon Barsacq had only contempt for the great Art Deco sets of the late twenties. "The moment Art Deco appears," he wrote, "everything seems false and outmoded."

But if many Americans were slow to accept Deco into their homes, they welcomed it in the movies. A trip to the movies could be a chance to leave behind such homey touches as antimacassars on chair arms, beaded lampshades, and ruffles on vanities. Modern design graced every aspect of motion picture exhibition, supplying

The lobby of Hollywood's Pantages Theatre, built in 1930, was used as a set for *The Good Fairy* five years later.

connotations of smartness and energy. Films could be seen in such modernistic movie palaces as the Pantages in Hollywood, the Warner in Erie, or the Paramount in Oakland, to name but a few.

Deco graphics permeated nearly every advertising campaign, even for war stories and westerns. Credit artwork and lettering were also a part of the Deco moviegoing experience, as were such details as the studio's logo. The Warner Brothers shield, for example, was fashionably angular during the early thirties, but 20th Century–Fox's trademark was the most Deco of all, seemingly ripped from the spires of the 1933 Chicago: A Century of Progress exposition. Not far behind was Universal's shimmering plexiglass globe which ushered in the studio's new administration during the Moderne second half of the decade.

The cartoon accompanying the feature might also have Art Deco elements. For example, Walt Disney gave his favorite canine a streamlined doghouse in "Pluto's Dream House" (1939). In 1936 Tex Avery directed a charming Merrie Melody for Warner Brothers called "Miss Glory," which bore the unusual credit "Modern Art conceived and designed by Leodora Cogdon." It was the Art Moderne dream of a rube bellhop—a vision of a swank hotel where svelte guests and employees performed a Busby Berkeley–style number to the tune of Harry Warren and Al Dubin's "Page Miss Glory."

Studio logos of the 1930s.

"MISS GLORY"
A MERRIE MELODY SONG CARTOON
VITAPHONE #3771
REL. N°1404

A
LEON
SCHLESINGER
CARTOON

Here's what admission to Radio City Music Hall would buy during the week of March 5, 1936 (in addition to the greatest Art Deco surroundings imaginable): the Music Hall Grand Organ, the Music Hall News, the Music Hall Symphony Orchestra, and a stage show entitled *2036: A Preview of the Future.* The show comprised four musical sketches entitled "Dawn of the New Century," "Scientific Creation," "Love Is Still the Same," and "Sunray Set-Ups." All of this was followed by Fred Astaire and Ginger Rogers co-starring in RKO's streamlined spectacular *Follow the Fleet.* After such Modernistic bombardment, there were surely patrons relieved to return home to a brick fireplace and doilies.

A Note on Attribution

Did Cedric Gibbons or Richard Day do the sets for *Our Dancing Daughters?* How much control did Van Nest Polglase really exert over the design for *Top Hat?* Movie credits won't answer these questions; attribution for art direction (and to a certain extent costume design) is almost impossible to pinpoint. We are dealing with corpo-

Warner Bros.' "Miss Glory," a Deco-influenced cartoon by Tex Avery from 1936.

(*Left*) This New York movie theater was specially redecorated to promote Warner Bros.' *Footlight* (1933).

rate entities, each of which had its own staff with its own modus operandi. What's more, many silents and early talkies, especially at Paramount, omitted art direction credits completely.

At most studios during the sound era, the art director featured most prominently in the credits was basically in a supervisory position. Since the head of the department couldn't perform all tasks adding up to a polished whole, authority was delegated. In *Hollywood in the Thirties*, John Baxter notes that "there were specialists in interiors, exteriors, ships, castles, nightclubs, Oriental buildings; a film requiring some or all of these would involve the talents of ten men, each making a major contribution which would receive no acknowledgement in the film's credits." RKO's Carroll Clark recalled as many as 110 men under his command handling such particulars as carpets and furniture. Polglase had five unit art directors (including Clark) with whom he devised the highly influential look of the Astaire-Rogers pictures. For those superproductions, each of the major sets had its own art director whose work had to be passed by Polglase.

To further muddy the waters for those researching who did what, there is the special role of "production designer." The term was invented by David O. Selznick to describe the work of William Cameron Menzies on *Gone With the Wind* (1939). In point of fact, Menzies had been making similar contributions for two decades: that is, actively working with the producer and director from a film's earliest stages to coordinate all visual elements, supervising other art directors, and indicating camera angles and lighting in detailed sketches. Men like Menzies were really associate directors.

Men like Cedric Gibbons were really executives. *Movie Facts and Feats* lists Gibbons as the filmmaker with the most screen credits (over 1,500 between 1917 and 1955). As head man, he felt he deserved mention for all of the work of his department. Beginning in 1924, the year of the company's organization, Gibbons's MGM contracts included a clause giving him sole credit for every film the studio produced in the United States.

Art director Preston Ames, who began working under Gibbons in 1936, describes their working relationship this way:

> Cedric Gibbons worked very closely with me, as he did with all his art directors. The best way to describe our operation is to compare it to an architect's office. You confer with the head man, but eventually you are assigned an architect who works on your assignment. The office, however, is going to be very much aware of whether the architect's work is in keeping with the experience, the style, and the creativity of the head man. If there was bad taste, if there was bad composition, or if it couldn't be photographed, Gibbons would spot it right off the bat and you were in trouble. If you did something which you thought was the proper thing to do and the director came along saying, "This isn't right,"

A striking set by William Cameron Menzies for *Cobra* (1925).

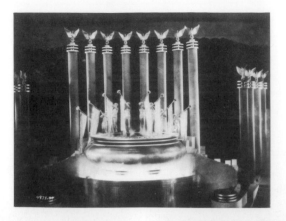

Preliminary sketch of Herman Rosse's modular set for the "Melting Pot" number from *The King of Jazz* (1930). Above are stills of the set in its various permutations.

A Woman of Affairs (1928), with Greta Garbo, John Gilbert, and Douglas Fairbanks, Jr.

Gibbons would defend you, or he might say, "It is a mistake." But if you were right you always had the support of your supervisor. He'd back you to the hilt. Gibbons had the background (I think that's the proper word) to have the great respect and admiration of the entire studio. He represented quality, and he represented good art direction.[1]

Working at movie studios meant being a team player, and many more independent artists simply could not adjust. Donald Oenslager, one of New York's most respected designers, spoke for many in his generation when he wrote:

> Many Broadway scene designers have been tempted by opportunities unlimited in the Elysian Fields of Cinema Land and also attracted (and why not?) by financial reward! But most who have journeyed west to labor in a major studio have returned home to Times Square as prodigal sons with the same disillusions. "No opportunity for individual expression," "assembly-line control," "design lost in the shuffle of production," "no life in it."[2]

Erté's tale was typical. In 1925, the celebrated designer and illustrator was wooed by Louis B. Mayer. MGM's grand plans for Erté's talents were promoted to the hilt; he was given an exact reproduction of his studio in France to work in, a chauffeured limousine, two French-speaking secretaries, and a lavish bungalow at the Beverly Hills Hotel. What he wasn't given was freedom. Months spent on Cu-

[1] Donald Knox, *The Magic Factory* (New York: Praeger, 1973).
[2] Donald M. Oenslager, *The Theatre of Donald Oenslager* (Middletown, Conn.: Wesleyan University Press, 1978).

bistic set designs for *Paris* were squandered when executives demanded a more traditional approach—and, despite his reputation, Lillian Gish rejected his costume sketches for *La Bohème*. It was a terribly frustrating year for Erté. His singular style, combining Art Nouveau and Art Deco, would have surely brought MGM the exoticism and flamboyance which made De Mille's Paramount productions so sensational.

Working for De Mille was no picnic either. C. B. not only believed in miracles, he expected his staff to perform them on a daily basis. High tension and low wages drove designers Wilfred Buckland and Paul Iribe away and Mitchell Leisen to a nervous breakdown. Arnold "Buddy" Gillespie worked as a draftsman on *Manslaughter* (1922) and was paid twenty-five dollars for a seven-day week, with an average work load of sixteen hours a day. During the mid-twenties, De Mille hired Broadway's Norman Bel Geddes, father of Barbara as well as the Streamline style. Egos clashed loudly on the set of *Feet of Clay* (1924). Bel Geddes, whose philosophy insisted that each detail be an organic outgrowth of the action, was appalled by the director's emphasis on ostentation. It was only under protest that he designed an overwhelmingly baroque mansion with peacocks populating its garden.

Newly recruited designers discovered that each studio had its own "look": the result of employees respecting the preferences of their bosses (producers, directors, or department heads). Cedric Gibbons loved decorative plaster and loathed wallpa-

Van Nest Polglase with RKO Art Department staff members.

(*Left*) Director Edmund Goulding and Douglas Fairbanks clowning between takes of *Reaching for the Moon* (1931).

per, an idiosyncrasy which helped define MGM's glossy style. As head of MGM's art department, Gibbons wielded tremendous power which spilled over to other departments as well: wardrobe, set dressing, matte painting, special effects, and photography. In fact, the studio's characteristic high-key photography was specifically designed to show off Gibbons's shiny white sets. Cinematographers like James Wong Howe who refused to flood the set with light answered to Gibbons. The story was the same at other studios. Set decorator Julia Heron learned shortly after going to work for Sam Goldwyn that he would scream if anything was seen on a wall behind an actor. Thus Goldwyn films like *Dodsworth* (1936) had a bare, white-on-white look.

By the mid-sixties, studios had lost not only their feudal power, but also consistent "looks." Gone were the days when a screen star like Miriam Cooper could pick up a fan magazine and discover that an overzealous publicist had credited her with the sets for *Serenade* (1921). The designer was actually William Cameron Menzies. Like so many others, Menzies accepted the rewards—as well as the limitations—of the studio system. That system had the resources to realize the most voluptuous fantasies of its designers, and to transport audiences to a world of impossible luxury.

An angular Leo the Lion, used for MGM promotional purposes.

Filming within the film *Movie Crazy* (1932), starring Harold Lloyd.

Anders Randolph and Greta Garbo in *The Kiss* (1929).

The Rich Are Always with Us

PARLOR, BEDROOM, AND BATH

During the decade following World War I, the American economy began to skyrocket. Nouveau riche families were climbing steadily up the social scale, casting off traditional attitudes and fashions like cocoons. A new moral and social code was forming, one which Frederick Lewis Allen referred to as a "revolution" in his classic history of the 1920s, *Only Yesterday:*

> Diverse influences—the post-war disillusion, the new status of women, the Freudian gospel, the automobile, Prohibition, the sex and confession magazines, and the movies—had their part in bringing about the revolution. Each of them, as an influence, was played upon by all the others; none of them could alone have changed to any great degree the folkways of America; together their force was irresistible.

Since the days of the nickelodeons, America had been going to the movies to see the fulfillment of its dreams. It was only to be expected that the upper classes would prove a focal point for popular entertainment. As the twenties took hold, movies began reflecting an opulence that suddenly seemed to be within closer reach than ever before. America was splurging, but even those too timid to live recklessly could at least emulate the affluent.

Times haven't changed. In previewing the 1984 television show "Glitter," the *New York Daily News* clucked, "The way television networks see it, most clods watching American TV will never own a Rolls-Royce, live in a mansion, or drink champagne from a jewel-encrusted slipper. But they can't get enough of people who do. Glitz, glamour, sparkle, fantasy."

One major result of the public's determination to sever its bonds with the re-

cent past was the emergence in the twenties of a visual style which the socially as-
cendant could adopt as an emblem. Quick to recognize and even influence trends,
Hollywood jumped on the Art Deco bandwagon. Here at last was a chance to create
sets that not only would be sumptuous and striking, but could also immediately de-
lineate the social attitudes of a film's characters. In Clarence Brown's *A Woman of
Affairs* (1928), John Gilbert's old-monied family resides in a mansion steeped in
taste, refinement, and traditional furnishings. In contrast, Greta Garbo and her
brother Douglas Fairbanks, Jr., are uninhibited young "moderns" whose mansion is
decorated in High Zigzag. MGM supervising art director Cedric Gibbons was responsible for these sets, and for a good deal more than that. It was Gibbons, more
than any other designer, who first fixed the place of the Art Deco visual vocabulary
in American cinema.

Handsome and poised, Gibbons concocted an image and lifestyle that made
him a Hollywood celebrity almost on a par with movie stars. In looks, dress, and de-
portment he was the paragon of male elegance. Mme. Elinor Glyn, high priestess of
Ruritanian romance in the twenties, begged him repeatedly to star in one of the
films made from her best-selling novels. Gibbons, she insisted, was among the select
few on her honor roll of people who had "It."

Gibbons was born in Brooklyn in 1893. Although his father headed a successful
architectural firm, Gibbons was never trained as an architect. In 1914 he entered
the film industry, as a set dresser to Hugo Ballin at the Edison Studios in New York.
Ballin was soon lured to Hollywood by Samuel Goldwyn, and took Gibbons with
him. Not long after his arrival, Ballin gave up art direction in order to produce and
direct. This allowed Gibbons to replace Ballin, taking the then-unheard-of title of
supervising art director.

During his years with Goldwyn, Gibbons banished all painted backdrops from
interior scenes. He insisted on naturally constructed sets, and soon became known as
the man who "put the glove on the mantelpiece"—an action impossible to perform
if the mantelpiece were merely a painted backdrop. Some constructed sets had already been in use by this time, but Gibbons was crucial in establishing them as the
rule rather than the exception. Already he was displaying his trademarks: lavishness
and high style.

When the Goldwyn company merged with the Metro and Mayer companies to
form MGM, Gibbons retained his title of supervising art director.[1] Shortly after-
ward, he attended the 1925 Exposition des Arts Décoratifs et Industriels Modernes
in Paris. The experience completely re-formed his artistic vision, and with the landmark *Our Dancing Daughters* (1928), he unveiled the spacious Art Deco style for
which he would become famous.

This film's chic, soaring Deco sets depicted a dream world of the well-to-do. It
formulated and fixed MGM's attitude toward its audiences. In his book *American
Silent Film*, William K. Everson states:

[1] His gifted staff of unit art directors included Ben Carré, Merrill Pye, Richard Day, and Arnold
Gillespie

MGM's films were always aimed at audiences that were rich—or (according to their own philosophy) poor audiences that *envied* the rich and thus wanted to see glamor and elegance in films rather than reality. The "average" MGM family was usually independently wealthy and lived in a mad whirl of cocktail parties aboard yachts, with the source of such unlimited income usually unspecified but taken for granted.

From the start, the studio knew that it had a film of major visual impact. A 1928 press release for *Our Dancing Daughters* trumpeted:

> Modernistic effects in furniture and architecture are being used with a vengeance by Metro-Goldwyn-Mayer in Joan Crawford's new picture. Weird beds, almost on the floor, have little woodwork frame save foot-high boards which conceal the springs and do away with the conventional legs of a bed. These are set against a wall whose only ornamenting is the shape of the doors. Black statues set against gold papered panels form the only ornamental note. The whole thing is being photographed under the huge new incandescent lights.

William Haines, an MGM star who became one of Hollywood's most successful interior decorators, visited the set and reacted with mild shock. "It looks," he said, "like someone had a nightmare while designing a church and tried to combine it with a Grauman theatre."

Our Dancing Daughters was wildly successful, and exerted a huge influence on American design as the country gleefully took up its Art Deco gospel. This romance of the Jazz Age provided an entirely new decorative style to match the up-to-the-minute modernity of its characters and plot. The film was so popular that it spawned two sequels, *Our Modern Maidens* (1929) and *Our Blushing Brides* (1930), both of which carried on the bold Art Deco scheme. By the time of *Our Blushing Brides*, critics had caught on to the psychology behind MGM's use of Deco. *The New York Times* review of August 2, 1930, read:

> All three girls [Joan Crawford, Anita Page, and Dorothy Sebastian] yearn for the trappings that make for a comfortable life, and the two who sacrifice their hall rooms for modernistic settings must pay the piper. Connie goes to her death by poison after her David, a social lion, has led her to believe that marriage is the pot of gold at the end of their premarital adventures. Francine becomes attached to one whom she believes a millionaire, but who is caught as a thief. Gerry, however, true to her principles, remains the paragon and profits in the end by marrying Tony Jardine, the son of the department store owner.

Tony has an astonishing Art Deco treehouse where he likes to go to "get away from it all." The review continues: "If by getting away from it all he means the angular settings that Cedric Gibbons has conceived, he is justified. Even the little studio in the tree, for example, when seen from inside, might have occupied a good portion of any armory."

The Big White Set (BWS), which became a hallmark of Van Nest Polglase's designs in the Astaire-Rogers films, was actually inaugurated by Gibbons. His Deco films of the late twenties had sets that boasted white as the dominant color factor, technically feasible because white sets could at long last be painted in true white. Arc lighting had been used in the past, which necessitated rendering the white parts of the set in pink or green. The effect on the finished film would otherwise have been blinding. With the newly developed incandescent lighting, true white could become the predominant element in a set. In addition, the new changes in film stock (from orthochromatic to the more sensitive panchromatic) lent the image a crisp glossiness ideal for Deco sets.

At the time Deco was in its transitional phase to Streamline Moderne, Hobart Erwin and Frederick Hope were designing *Dinner at Eight* at MGM. The set for the Jean Harlow–Wallace Beery residence utilized few Deco elements save the overwhelming, almost overpowering whiteness that had become Gibbons's trademark. Whether or not the design scheme was in the best of taste (Beery and Harlow were playing a bratty nouveau riche couple), it certainly was striking. Soon to be known as the "white telephone" look, it framed a platinum-haired, white-gowned, white-skinned Jean Harlow in an orgy of white decor—eleven shades in all. In addition, Harlow's close-ups were filmed through haystacks of white gauze. Small wonder cameraman William H. Daniels was driven mad coping with the intricacies of so much whiteness in one set.

Gibbons's enthusiasm for Art Deco made him a leader of contemporary tastes. During the early years of his career, he had tended to consider the design of both period and modern films to be little more than journeyman work of a reconstructive nature. With the new modernistic design at his disposal, he could take his imagination far beyond the realm of the representational.

The decorating craze touched off by *Our Dancing Daughters* was unprecedented. Households began aping Gibbons's use of such elements as venetian blinds, dancing figurines, and indirect lighting. Those with money and relatively adventurous tastes were soon having their homes redecorated in the "modern" style. Unfortunately, few of these homes could fully capture the scale and luxury of Gibbons's sets, which tended to depict drawing rooms roughly the size of Grand Central Station.

The home which Gibbons shared with his wife Dolores Del Rio was designed with as much Art Deco flair as any of his sets. Gibbons's office at MGM, designed by Merrill Pye, was also a Deco showplace. In effect, Gibbons was leading an Art Deco life worthy of a character in an MGM film. By night he entertained Hollywood nobility in his modern mansion in the Santa Monica mountains; by day he repaired to his streamlined office to preside over his staff of hundreds. Designer Herbert Ryman, who joined MGM in 1932 as a sketch artist, described him as existing

> . . . in a kind of aura, or nimbus. He would arrive in his Dusenberg, in the grey homburg hat and the grey gloves, and he would walk up the stairs to the Art Department. By the time he was on the landing, one glove was off and his grey homburg was swept off, and he would walk in and say good morning to his secretary, with all of us in the art department watching him appear and disappear with this elegant procedure. I think it was intended on his part.[2]

Across town on the Paramount lot, the residences of the rich were depicted with a more Continental flair. As with most Hollywood products of the time, the Depression was virtually ignored. Lavish settings were the rule, and the Art Deco suites in such films as *One Hour With You* (1932), *Monte Carlo* (1930), and *Safety in Numbers* (1930) were stunners. Paramount's supervising art director Hans Dreier had served his apprenticeship at the UFA-EFA studios in Germany. He brought with him a European sensibility as well as a Bauhaus-grounded espousal of teamwork, practical creative education, and artistic unity. Many of Paramount's other key directors and technicians were also European—UFA-EFA, renowned and powerful, was Paramount's sister studio and a proving ground for stars and filmmakers who later moved on to Hollywood.

Dreier reigned as Paramount's supervising art director until 1950. But unlike Cedric Gibbons, Dreier also maintained his métier as a practicing designer. He made considerable contributions to the bulk of the studio's product, but also was willing to share the credit. Most of his post-1932 films bear collaborative art direction credits with his assistants and unit art directors. He was also the first supervising art director to regularly visit architectural and design colleges in search of new talent.

"Hans Dreier was a very military figure, a disciplinarian," says designer Boris Leven. "But at the same time he believed in freedom; he wanted you to develop your own way." Roland Anderson, who worked under Dreier for nearly twenty years, said, "Of all the art directors I have known in this town, Hans was the greatest teacher. I learned everything I know from Hans."

It was Ernst Lubitsch who first convinced Dreier to join him at Paramount in 1923. It was for Lubitsch that Dreier provided some of his most inspired work. Three of their collaborations, *Monte Carlo* (1930), *One Hour With You* (1932), and *Trouble in Paradise* (1932), were strongly influenced by Art Deco.

Monte Carlo takes place primarily in a Deco hotel where Jeanette MacDonald is pursued by Jack Buchanan. The sets are irresistible: even the wallpaper in the hotel suite is a riot of Art Deco design. *One Hour With You* is freer from the technical constraints of the early talkie period. Lubitsch's camera pans and tracks

[2] John Hambley and Patrick Downing, *The Art of Hollywood* (London: Thames Television, 1979).

through the Art Deco home of Jeanette MacDonald and Maurice Chevalier, even following this married couple directly into bed.

Trouble in Paradise is considered by many to be a high point of sophistication in thirties cinema. All three main characters—two of them professional crooks—have an offhanded attitude toward sex. Kay Francis's mansion, where much of the action takes place, was designed by Dreier as a blend of Art Deco and Bauhaus. (Dreier even included Bauhaus furniture from his own residence in the film's sets.) The decorative mixture produced a distillation of style which nearly made the mansion the fourth leading character.

Ernst Lubitsch was one of Paramount's two top directors during the 1930s; the other was Cecil B. De Mille. Such was De Mille's power that he commandeered his own production unit at the studio, and made his movies the way *he* saw fit. De Mille was as responsible for the look of his films as any art director, but he knew the value of a good art director, and tried to work with the best. He was the first director to lure a major stage designer (Wilfred Buckland) to work in the cinema. Cedric Gibbons called Wilfred Buckland "the first man of recognized ability to forsake the theatre for the motion picture, and to him are attributed the first consistent and

Jeanette MacDonald and Maurice Chevalier in *One Hour With You.*

well-designed motion picture sets. He brought to the screen a knowlege of mood and a dramatic quality which until then had been totally lacking."

De Mille was a style unto himself; he transcended Art Deco, although Art Deco elements were often a part of that style. Most significantly, by importing designer Paul Iribe from France in the early twenties, he became one of the first American filmmakers to introduce aspects of the new French decorative art.

Unfairly characterized today as a naïve Bible-thumper, De Mille actually enjoyed quite a different reputation during the first two decades of his career. The contemporary comedy-dramas he produced at that time revealed him to be a director of trailblazing sophistication—a glorifier of opulence and sensuality, dubbed "the High Priest of savoir-faire" by Anita Loos.

Mitchell Leisen, one of De Mille's most inventive designers and later a director himself, had this to say about De Mille's approach: "For the type of thing he did, he was very good. De Mille had no nuances. Everything was in neon lights six feet tall: LUST, REVENGE, SEX. You had to learn to think the way he thought, in capital letters."

Bebe Daniels (*center*) in *Reaching for the Moon* (1930), released by United Artists.

Certainly a major heading emblazoned in capital letters was LUXURY. With the upgrading of movie theatres in the late 1910s, middle-class audiences became habitual moviegoers. De Mille seized on their desire to see how the other half lived, and exploited the much-publicized loosening of morals following World War I. When De Mille's characters sinned, they sinned in style.

Never one to bypass titillation, De Mille put bathrooms on the map. He turned them into fabulous resorts of shimmering marble, onyx, tile, and chrome, with fuzzy oversize towels and rugs for textural contrast. In addition, taps over the tub gushed rose water or milk for those bored with mere water. Naturally, such fetishism became a joke. Included in the catalog of a plumbing manufacturer was a plush tub labeled "Early De Mille." But being known as "the plumber's best friend" didn't seem to annoy the showman; ridicule, after all, was publicity. As he wrote in his autobiography: "I do not shy away from the fact that bathtubs and bathrooms have appeared in many of my pictures; and if the modern American bathroom is a clean and comfortable part of the American home, my pictures may have had something to do with that wholesome development."

The American Legion of Decency didn't find the bathroom Wilfred Buckland created for De Mille's *Male and Female* (1919) the least bit wholesome. The organization viewed the entire bathroom sequence as merely an excuse to ceremoniously undress Gloria Swanson, who, with the aid of two maids, was eased into a sunken tub as the camera lingered on her bare back. It took a number of takes before the star was sufficiently relaxed. "Prolong it!" yelled De Mille. "Relish the smell of the rose water! More rapture; make the fans feel like they are going down with you!"

The scene was a wow, spawning similar sequences in which lovely female bodies enacted the ritual of preparing for a party or rendezvous. Such florid detail revolutionized interior decoration, and soon plumbing firms were taking full-page ads to market bathroom fixtures modeled on De Mille's modern wonders.

(*Male and Female* did not actually present De Mille's first bathroom. That honor went to *Old Wives for New* [1918], in which Elliott Dexter played a sensitive husband saddled with a wife whose messy bathroom reflected a generally slothful attitude. One look at Florence Vidor's gleaming bathroom and he knew she was ideal.)

While the public devoured De Mille's palatial version of marriage and divorce, critics were divided. *Photoplay* called *Feet of Clay* (1924) "a pearl onion in a platinum setting." Burns Mantle in the same magazine proclaimed *Why Change Your Wife?* (1920) "the most gorgeously sensual film of the month; in decoration the most costly, in physical allure the most fascinating, in effect the most immoral."

Dynamite, made at MGM in 1929, drew attention for its use of wildly stylized Art Deco sets. Charles Dranton in his review in the *New York World* wrote: "Bizarre is, I believe, the word for the house furnishings to which the heroine is addicted. Seeing things as they are in her dizzy establishment you seem to see Greenwich Vil-

1398-53

Kay Francis and Herbert Marshall in *Trouble in Paradise*, designed by Hans Dreier.

lage come into money." On the other hand, the anonymous critic for the *Detroit News* was enchanted:

> No review of a De Mille picture is complete without some reference to his bathtub exhibition. Cecil offers one in this picture that will make every master plumber cry out for sheer joy. It is a gold tub, with black onyx trimmings, and shimmering mirrors replace the ordinary tiling. There are also many other smart tricks in home furnishings to show that the director, although busy probing religious themes, has kept abreast of modern house-keeping.

Not to be left out, screen stars turned their bathrooms into De Millian sets. Many a housewife decided to redecorate after reading about Charles Ray's $75,000 cut-glass bathtub, Gloria Swanson's golden tub surrounded by black marble, or Pola Negri's giant Roman plunge. Eyebrows were also raised by Lilyan Tashman's toilet seat upholstered in sable. Disappointingly, De Mille's own bathroom was a no-frills affair.

Needless to say, there was never a suggestion in the movies that bathrooms were for anything but bathing. The sole exception was King Vidor's realist masterpiece *The Crowd* (1928), whose shot of a commode so angered Louis B. Mayer that he carried on for years about the disgrace of having a "human function" in a Metro movie.

Even bathing was curtailed with the toughened Production Code of 1934. One of the few late-thirties bathtub scenes to pass the censors was in *The Women* (1939). There are several explanations as to why Joan Crawford was allowed to wallow in bubbles. The scene was already well-known from the highly successful play; it made the important plot point that Crawford's character had a private bathroom phone for the sole purpose of speaking to her lover; and in addition every effort was made to keep the scene within the limits of "good taste." Crawford remained stationary—no breast-bobbing here—and bubbles were discreetly arranged for maximum coverage.

The set of her bathroom, on the other hand, was a monument to bad taste—just right for the vulgar social climber she played. Twelve-year-old Virginia Weidler had the privilege of tossing off the scene's last line: "And *another* thing. I think this bathroom is perfectly ridiculous!"

Blackmailer Evelyn Brent's lair from *Interference* (1929).

Safety in Numbers (1930) with Charles "Buddy" Rogers, Roscoe Karns, Carole Lombard, Kathryn Crawford, and Josephine Dunn.

Claudette Colbert (*right,* in white evening gown) in *Honor Among Lovers* (1931).

"The Latest in Fountains" from *The Magnificent Flirt* (1928).

Monroe Owsley, Frank McHugh, and Bette Davis in *Ex-Lady* (1933).

Celebrated International Style architect Paul Nelson was hired by Gloria Swanson to design her comedy vehicle *What a Widow!* (1930).

Warner Bros. set test still for *Recaptured Love* (1930).

Robert Montgomery and Joan Crawford in the "little tree house" from *Our Blushing Brides* (1930).

Lilyan Tashman (left) attends a wild party in *New York Nights* (1929).

The Cedric Gibbons style is exemplified in these set test stills from the Greta Garbo vehicle *The Single Standard* (1929).

Gibbons glamour: Petting party and wedding party in *Our Modern Maidens* (1929).

Joan Crawford dallies with Rod La Rocque, but ultimately marries Douglas Fairbanks, Jr.

The Marx Brothers invade Margaret Dumont's Long Island mansion in *Animal Crackers* (1930).

Children of Pleasure (1930).

Cary Grant, Roland Young, and Constance Bennett in *Topper* (1937).

Set test stills from MGM's *Five and Ten* (1931).

Mitchell Leisen, later to become a director, designed this posh setting for Cecil B. De Mille's *Dynamite* (1929). The decorative panel hanging above Charles Bickford and Kay Johnson is Jean Dupas's *Les Perruches,* a focal point of the Pavillon du Collectionneur at the 1925 Paris Exposition.

The stars of *Scandal Sheet* (1931), Clive Brook and Kay Francis.

Set sketch and set test shot from *Top Hat* (1935), starring Fred Astaire and Ginger Rogers, supervised by Van Nest Polglase.

Loretta Young in *The Magnificent Flirt* (1928).

Groucho Marx on his throne/bed in the mythical kingdom of Fredonia in *Duck Soup* (1933).

860-67

440-4

Cedric Gibbons could lampoon the very style he had created. The 1928 studio caption for this still reads: "Drammer as portrayed in the movies. Marion Davies and Paul Ralli pull a Gilbert-Garbo for a comedy sequence in MGM's *Show People*, which King Vidor directs."

Greta Garbo in *The Kiss* (1929).

Sleeping arrangements: Married couples usually kept separate beds in the movies, even before the imposition of the Production Code in 1934. This often resulted in a pleasing mirror-image effect: Jack Mulhall and Patsy Ruth Miller in *Twin Beds* (1929); Gloria Swanson and Laurence Olivier in *Perfect Understanding* (1933).

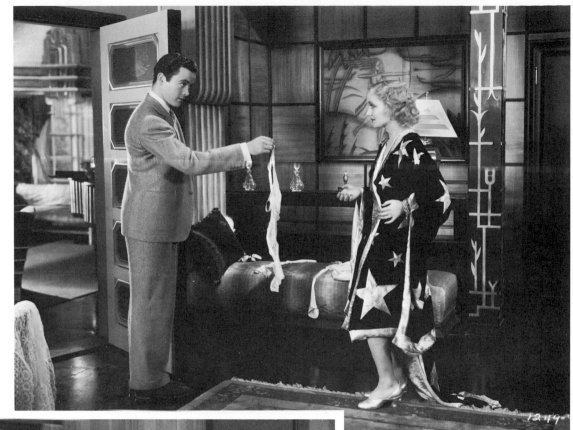

Charles "Buddy" Rogers and Carole Lombard in *Safety in Numbers* (1930).

Wife vs. mistress: Irene Dunne (*right*), confronts Mae Murray (*left*), in her husband's *Bachelor Apartment* (1931).

Pauline Starke's boudoir is a jumbled nightmare of Art Deco overkill in *Women Love Diamonds* (1927). "Good girls" had more refined taste!

Clark Gable and Joan Crawford in *Possessed* (1931).

The design of *What Price Beauty* (1928) reveals the hand of Natacha Rambova, credited as the film's screenwriter.

Betty Stockfield bored with her lot in life in *Captivation,* made in Britain in 1931.

Fred Hope and Hobart Erwin designed the nouveau riche boudoir of Jean Harlow and Wallace Beery in *Dinner at Eight* (1934), creating the "white telephone" look that was to reign in Hollywood for nearly ten years.

Jeanette MacDonald in *Monte Carlo* (1930).

Cecil B. De Mille directed and Paul Iribe designed *The Affairs of Anatol* (1921), in which Satan Synne (Bebe Daniels) has a "bat" boudoir and favors octopus gowns.

A Joseph Urban setting for *Doctors' Wives* (1931), starring Joan Bennett and Warner Baxter.

Kay Francis in *Girls About Town* (1931).

D.F.-4200-A.19

Douglas Fairbanks attended by Edward Everett Horton in his bachelor apartment from *Reaching for the Moon* (1931).

Charles Bickford in Cecil B. De Mille's *Dynamite* (1929).

Original MGM studio caption: "Cecil B. De Mille shows Kay Johnson the technique of 'crowning' Charles Bickford with a glass bottle in *Dynamite*."

Charles Bickford scrutinizes Kay Johnson's gold-and-cut-glass bathtub in *Dynamite*.

Tallulah Bankhead in *Faithless* (1932).

Paramount supervising art director
Hans Dreier.

Cedric Gibbons (*left*) confers with
associate Fred Hope.

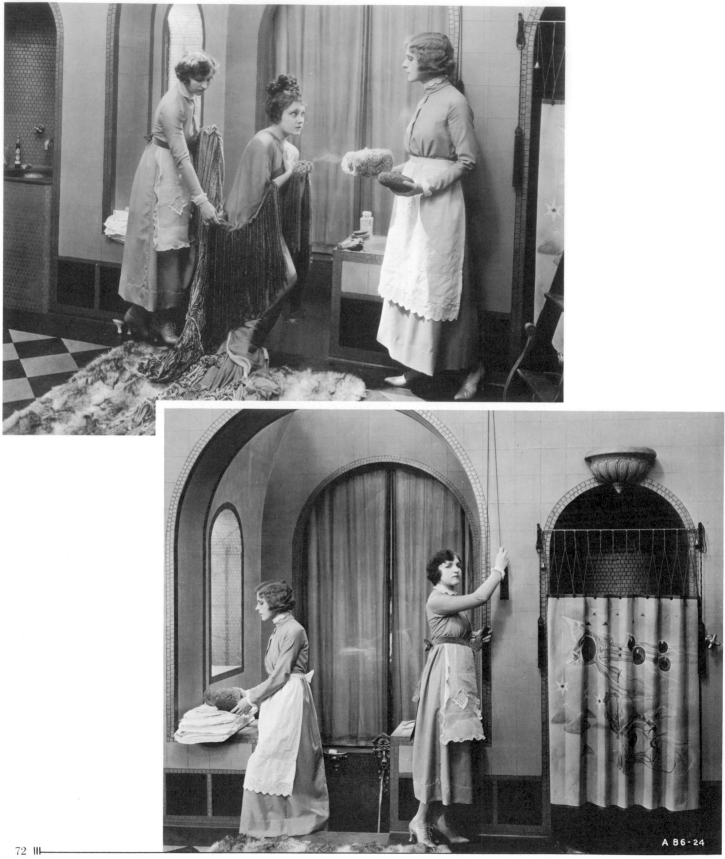

Two views of Gloria Swanson's notorious bathroom in Cecil B. De Mille's *Male and Female* (1919).

"Singin' in the Bathtub" from Warner Bros.' *The Show of Shows* (1929).

In *Annabelle's Affairs* (1931), Jeanette MacDonald receives Sally Blane and Joyce Compton from her bathtub.

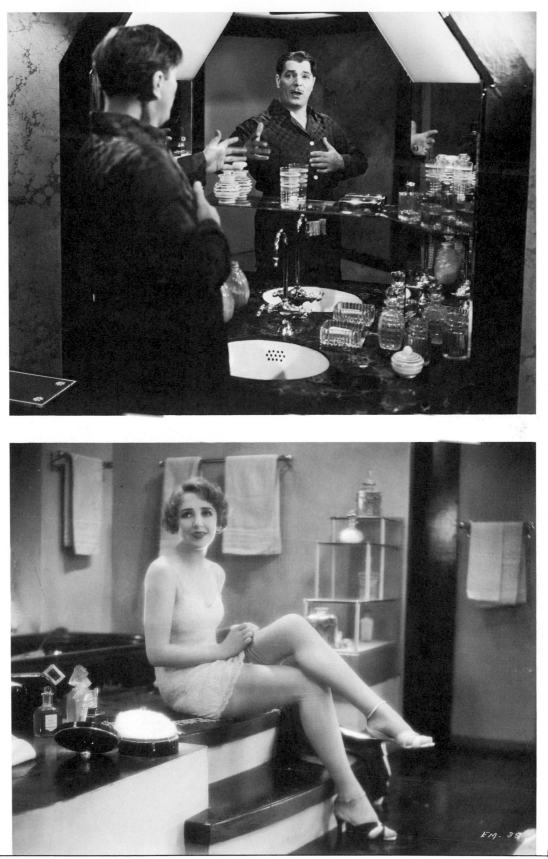

Warner Baxter vocalizes in *Wife, Husband and Friend* (1938).

Bebe Daniels in *My Past* (1931).

"MODERNISM ENTERS THE BATH. . . . Milady's bath, the latest idea in interior architecture for the American home, being shown for the first time on the screen in Florence Vidor's new Paramount production 'The Magnificent Flirt.' " (*original studio caption*)

1133-2/4

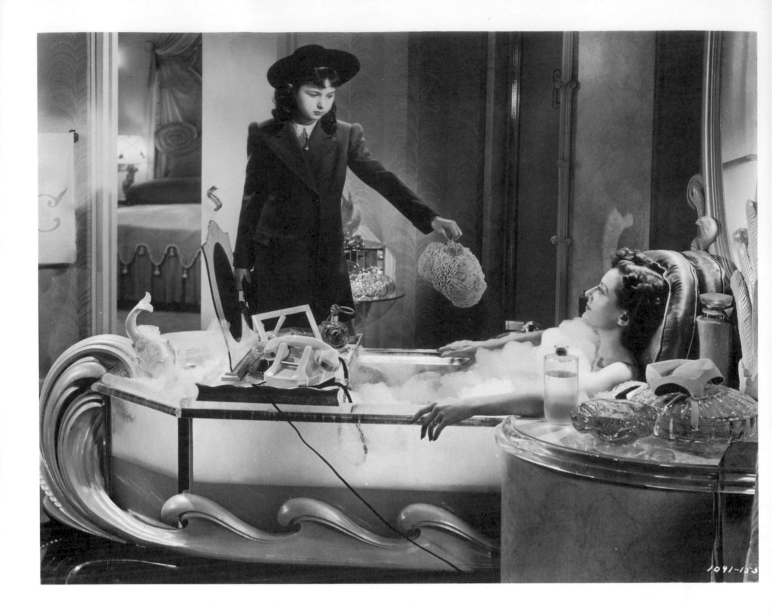

The tub from which Joan Crawford greeted Virginia Weidler in *The Women* (1939) was recycled for Carl "Alfalfa" Switzer in the *Our Gang* short "Alfalfa's Double."

265-6-8

Ruth Chatterton, Ferdinand Gottschalk, and Gavin Gordon in *Female* (1933).

Success at Any Price

PLACES OF BUSINESS

Skylines changed with dizzying swiftness after World War I. The skyscraper boom between 1924 and 1931 introduced multicolored, stepped-back, triumphantly vertical masses of stone, terra cotta, brick, and metal. Although Art Deco was conceived as a popular style, it nevertheless offended traditional sensibilities. Screen exposure, however, did much to familiarize the public with modern architecture. Seeing stars doing glamorous things in Deco buildings removed much of the sting. What better way to ballyhoo the Empire State Building than to have King Kong climb it?

The towers of Manhattan stood for twentieth-century excitement to moviegoers worldwide. In Hollywood movies, it seemed inconceivable that the view from a New York window did not encompass the skyline. Back projection and painted backdrops fulfilled the expectations of the public. Hundreds of films opened with establishing shots of the great skyscrapers of the late twenties and early thirties. The shots were usually blandly assembled, but there were notable exceptions. *Street Scene* (1931) begins with a remarkable tilt shot which links the spires of Manhattan with a squalid slum below. *Dead End* (1937) opens with a brilliant montage of big-city sights and sounds. Both sequences, incidentally, are accompanied by Alfred Newman's Gershwinesque blues.

The Depression severely curtailed new construction of commercial buildings, but so many thirties movies glorified skyscrapers that it was easy for audiences to forget the balloon had burst. Hollywood kept the Gotham myth alive. It seemed the most natural thing in the world for Joan Crawford in *Possessed* (1931) to leave the factory and come to New York, where, on her first day, Clark Gable offered her a life of sinful refinement high in the clouds. Clearly, individual initiative could lick poverty any day of the week, at least in New York.

During this period, offices acquired glamour and sex appeal. The work force swelled with young women and any situation which brought opposite sexes and opposite classes together naturally had dramatic possibilities. Peeking through the windows of offices and shops was a favorite pastime for twenties and thirties screenwriters. And not only in Hollywood. *Osaka Elegy*, a Japanese production directed by Kenji Mizoguchi in 1936, begins with a shot of a Deco office building as a mournful arrangement of "Stairway to the Stars" is heard on the soundtrack. Once again a girl is led down the primrose path by a man in a position of power—a fate shared by such American soul sisters as Constance Bennett, Sylvia Sidney, Helen Twelvetrees, Margaret Sullavan, and Kay Francis. Whether such stories are tales of sexual harassment or soap opera depends on one's views on melodrama, yet their social significance is undeniable.

Called "confession movies" after the *True Confessions* school of literature, these films were most popular during the early years of the Depression. Women responded sympathetically to stories of working girls forced to use their bodies. Until movie censorship was strictly enforced in 1934, the relationship between sex and money was explicit. Nowhere was it blunter than in *Baby Face* (1933), in which Barbara Stanwyck cold-bloodedly climbed the corporate ladder, man by man, straight to the executive suite. The ad campaign summed it up: "SHE used everything SHE had . . . to get everything MEN had. . . . She stopped at nothing and made 'IT' pay."

These women used offices, shops, and factories as springboards to more exciting lives as Cinderellas or Magdalenes: economically upgraded and/or morally degraded. Judging by their Deco penthouses, the wages of sin could be most comforting. The captains of industry, whose charm and checkbooks wooed the heroines, had magnificent offices whose modernity mocked the gray spaces in which their minions toiled.

Movies, of course, caricatured extremes to make points more clearly. The vast, unvarying arrangement of desks in the Ernst Lubitsch sequence of *If I Had a Million* (with Charles Laughton, 1933) suggests stifling regimentation. Small wonder Laughton blows a raspberry in the face of the boss of bosses once he gets news of his impending fortune. Nearly thirty years later, Billy Wilder was to pay homage to Lubitsch with the office set in *The Apartment*.

Besides confession films, another genre which used office sets evocatively was the "rise and fall" film. *Citizen Kane* (1941) was a late entry in this cycle, which was most popular in the early thirties. The lesson that riches didn't bring happiness must have been comforting for those on breadlines. Here the glossy coldness of Deco provided a visual corollary for the barrenness of lives lived for money alone. Among the morally bankrupt moguls dwarfed by offices and boardrooms were Spencer

The Manhattan skyline is admired by the Hardy family in *Andy Hardy Meets Debutante* (1940).

Chester Conklin and Charlie Chaplin in Charles D. Hall's factory set for *Modern Times* (1936).

Tracy in *The Power and the Glory* (1933), Franchot Tone in *The World Moves On* (1934), Paul Muni in *The World Changes* (1933), Richard Barthelmess in *A Modern Hero* (1934), and Douglas Fairbanks, Jr., in *Success at Any Price* (1934). With *Female* (1933), Ruth Chatterton proved that women could be just as ruthless and miserable as men.

Art Deco can indeed be forbidding. The medical institute designed by Richard Day for *Arrowsmith* (1931) has the feel and dimensions of a criminal court. Although idealistic doctor Ronald Colman is initially impressed by this complex, the decor's disturbing impersonality makes his decision to leave more understandable. Likewise, the stern contours of John Barrymore's law office in *Counselor-at-Law* (1933) reflect the establishment values he has uneasily adopted rather than his own warmth and humanity.

Arrowsmith, although shorn of the exposé element of Sinclair Lewis's original novel, was but one of many films to dramatize conflicts within the medical profession. The clash between serving humanity and catering to the rich appears in such movies as *Symphony of Six Million* (1932) and *The Citadel* (1938), where imposingly modern offices symbolize selling out. Laboratories also provided opportunities for imaginative art direction, as in *Doctors' Wives* (1931), designed by Joseph Urban, which, like *Dinner at Eight* (1933), seemed to confirm the public's suspicion that doctors were really wolves in white. Hollywood also scrutinized psychiatrists, giving them splendid suites, as in *Desire* (1936).

Movies seldom reflected actual modern trends in the construction of department stores and factories. Art Deco establishments such as Bloomingdale's in midtown Manhattan or Wrigley's Long Island City chewing-gum plant were far less orthodox than most of their movie counterparts. Movies with working-class heroes or heroines deliberately deglamorized their working conditions to create greater class polarization. If Cinderella's counter or workbench were streamlined, there would be no sense of triumph when she wowed 'em at the nightclub, the boss's office, or his bachelor apartment.

Olive Borden in the fashion salon from *Fig Leaves* (1926). An early example of the use of Art Deco in a Hollywood set.

Hollywood's version of broadcasting lived up to radio's image as the marvel of the age. This studio is from *Danger on the Air* (1938).

Judge Claude Gillingwater is amused by the talents of Shirley Temple and Jimmy Durante in *Little Miss Broadway* (1938).

Fred MacMurray avoids Zasu Pitts at the airport in *13 Hours by Air* (1936).

(*Overleaf*) The Goldwyn Girls perform "Bend Down, Sister" in the International Style rooftop gymnasium of *Palmy Days* (1931).

Luxury hotels: Fred Astaire and Ginger Rogers performing "The Continental" in *The Gay Divorcee* (1934).

Lew Cody in *Adam and Evil* (1927).

Production still from *Grand Hotel* (1932).

Detail of above.

Retail wonderlands: Dixie Lee in *Redheads on Parade* (1935).

Jean Muir and John Boles in *Orchids to You* (1935).

Maureen O'Sullivan and Thomas Meehan in *Skyline* (1931).

Walter Huston's office overlooking his International Style factory in *Dodsworth* (1936).

Walter Huston and Kay Francis in *Gentlemen of the Press* (1929).

Franchot Tone in *The World Moves On* (1934).

A painted perspective from *Arrowsmith* (1931).

Clark Gable's office from *Wife Vs. Secretary* (1936).

Early talkies were often filmed in multiple versions for foreign release. In *The Easiest Way* (1931), Constance Bennett shows her stuff to boss Adolphe Menjou, while Lili Damita does the same for André Luguet in the French version, *Quand on est belle*.

Beatrice Lillie and minions in *Are Your There?* (1930).

Esther Dale and Claude Rains in *Crime Without Passion* (1934).

Doris Kenyon and John Barrymore in *Counsellor-at-Law* (1933).

Five and Ten (1931).

Douglas Fairbanks in *Reaching for the Moon* (1931).

Eleanor Powell in *Broadway Melody of 1936* (released 1935).

New York Nights

NIGHTCLUBS

Nightclubs boomed in the late twenties, boosted by both Prohibition and the changing moral tone. Despite regular raids and temporary closings, the best clubs managed to remain successful well into the 1930s. Broadway columnist Louis Sobol says in *The Longest Street:* "It was in saloons that I met for the first time statesmen, cinema beauties, generals, mobsters, society queens, chorus girls—even a future President of the United States. Public enemies, songwriters, authors, politicians—it was chiefly in the restaurants or night spots that I first came to know them."

The greatest Deco nightclubs did not appear until the early thirties, when it became apparent that the end of Prohibition was near. In May of 1933 *The Architectural Forum* featured an article entitled "Beer: Bars and Cafés," inspired by the government's decision to allow weak beer to be sold. The article pointed out:

> In European countries where the consumption of intoxicating liquors has not been a matter of police control, the fine art of designing and building bars has gone on apace with the rest of modern architecture. Bar rooms have put off, for the most part, their gaudy trappings, their mahogany cupids and garlands, and have acquired new character and elegance through simplicity of design. Since architecture today is a sort of nude and "functional" thing, our bars, being haunts of a sort of mental and emotional nudism, need not disguise their function any more than their whereabouts. The instrumentalities for drink should be forthright and obvious.

The dream clubs of the movies had few real-life equivalents. Texas Guinan's, El Morocco, the Rainbow Room—these were only springboards for the fantastic and grandiose plans of Hollywood's set designers. Here is Stephen Graham's eyewitness account of Texas Guinan's legendary twenties watering hole:

> The room is long, but not too long to be homely. No one can be lost in it. The walls are covered with pleated cloth and the roof tented with the same cloth softly toned in old rose, green and sere yellow. There are hanging Chinese lanterns, and on the walls illuminated designs of parrots. There are twenty or thirty tables and a small space in the middle of them for intimate dancing. There is nothing to try the eyes or irritate one. It is radiantly lighted and yet it is not the light associated with noisy excitement and jazz. You have come there not for a giddy hour but for hours and hours. That is why the illumination is so carefully toned.[1]

Did those twenty or thirty tables in a long tented room really make up the most famous club of the Prohibition era?

Only in rare cases were the fantasy clubs of the movies matched by reality. Ziegfeld's celebrated designer Joseph Urban created the Park Avenue Club, which featured soaring curvilinear walls covered with kaleidoscopically fragmented strips of mirrored glass. During the club's short life much of its decor, including its circular silver-and-chromium bar, was smashed and carted off by Prohibition officials.

Another Deco-influenced nightclub, the Town Casino, boasted a bar of sanded glass illuminated by sea-green lights with electric fountains placed behind it. Other fountains throughout the club had canopies and side panels of inlaid wood and blue neon, topped by geometric nude statues. Although the majority of New York speakeasies were smallish hideaways in private residences, Hollywood chose to focus on these larger modernistic dance-and-drink arenas that catered to those untouched by the Depression.

According to Hollywood, nightclubs were vast modern temples where passion and pleasure could be played out on a grand scale. Here, love affairs began and ended; fortunes were made and lost with a spin of the roulette wheel. Human lives might collapse, but the orchestra kept playing and the crowds kept dancing on and on and on . . .

Nightclub sets could provide any film with an injection of elegance. They were an instant excuse to put characters into tuxedos and formal gowns and remove them from the confines of office, apartment, or mansion. Invariably people who had been studiously trying to avoid each other would meet face-to-face in nightclub scenes— just barely containing shock, anger, and mortification under the rules of proper etiquette. But, of course, liquor served to loosen tongues and social decorum was often left at the coat check. Newly divorced Cary Grant and Irene Dunne accidentally met in the nightclub scene of Leo McCarey's *The Awful Truth* (1937). Romantic rivals might also meet, turning a location like the ladies' lounge at the Casino Roof in *The Women* (1939) into a stadium for back-stabbing bitchery. Nick and Nora Charles

---

[1] Stephen Graham, *New York Nights* (New York: George H. Doran, 1927).

knew they would always catch suspects at nightclubs in the *Thin Man* series, and even a Countess could be confronted by a Comrade in the Paris nightclub of *Ninotchka* (1939). *Wonder Bar* (1934) was set almost entirely in a nightclub. In its twenty-four-hour time frame it offered a little of everything—adultery, murder, swindling, suicide, plus Busby Berkeley musical numbers.

Nightclub scenes tended to be brief during the silent period; their dances and floor shows needed a sound track for full effectiveness. It was with the advent of the talkies that movie nightclubs made their first real impact. *Broadway*, by Philip Dunning and George Abbott, one of the big hits of the 1926–27 theatrical season, was filmed by Universal as its first all-talkie in 1929. The stage version had taken place entirely in the private party room of a small, seedy New York nightclub. When Hollywood got its hands on *Broadway*, this dingy cabaret turned into one of the most unbelievably lavish Art Deco sets ever built. Art director Charles D. Hall's creation was so vast that a special crane was constructed to allow the camera to swoop and glide, scrutinizing the set from every possible angle.

The film's pressbook grandly intoned that "they [Universal chief Carl Laemmle, Jr., and director Paul Fejos] envisioned a night club which should be symbolic not only of one of Broadway's glittering pleasure palaces, not only of Broadway itself, but of New York as a whole." Among the explosion of stylized geometric motifs were such elements as a weirdly glowing omniscient eye, an ocean liner, and forests of skyscrapers tilting at wild angles. Six towering light standards were in the form of skyscrapers illuminated with thousands of lights representing windows. Even a lighted elevated train roared over a cantilevered arch above the performers' entrance.

The term *Art Deco* had not yet been coined in 1929, so the Universal pressbook referred to the set as "a perfect example of ultra-modern cubistic art as a whole." One and a half million was cited as the cost of the set. Certainly this was the nightclub to end all nightclubs, yet the film's characters were always whining about breaking out of cheap joints like this and "seeing our names in lights!" In its review of May 28, 1929, *The New York Times* stated: "There are moments when one wishes that he [Fejos] had not enriched the night club atmosphere to the extent that he has, but after the film has been running for several minutes one becomes accustomed to the spacious settings, as well as the skyscraper costumes of the dancers and the straight line furnishings." Everyone, including the critics, succumbed to the insane opulence of this landmark Art Deco set.

An even more cavernous nightclub—but one built along starker lines—formed the centerpiece of Busby Berkeley's "Lullaby of Broadway" number in *Gold Diggers of 1935*. Conceived with an eye toward surrealism, this penthouse pleasure dome was built upon a series of stairways stretching out to infinity. Platoons of dancers flooded in to tap out "Lullaby of Broadway" while Wini Shaw and Dick Powell perched high above them atop a column which supported the only table in the en-

746-1

Joseph Urban's Park Avenue club (1931), one of New York's few great Art Deco nightclubs.

Edmund Lowe (*center*) as *King Solomon of Broadway* (1935).

tire room. The dream logic of the sequence veered into nightmare when Wini Shaw plunged to her death from the club's balcony.

Anton Grot's monumental set for this number went far beyond Art Moderne. In its starkness and lack of ornament, it evoked German Expressionism, and brought forth echoes of the solidly geometric stage designs of Max Reinhardt's German productions of the previous decade. Coincidentally, Reinhardt was working at the Warner Brothers studios in Hollywood in 1935, having been signed to co-direct *A Midsummer Night's Dream* with William Dieterle.

Swing Time, made by RKO the following year, was perhaps the ultimate nightclub film of the thirties. This Depression romance allowed a penniless Fred Astaire to dance and gamble his way into money, success, and Ginger Rogers' arms. Their progress was charted as they made their way through three penthouse nightclubs, each more spectacular than the one before. First was the Silver Sandal, impressive enough on its own terms with its chrome-against-white decor and tables on curved tiers. This club was named after the Silver Slipper on West Forty-eighth Street, which had been one of New York's best-known nightclubs until its closing in 1932.

The other two nightclubs, the Club Raymond and the redecorated Silver Sandal, were designed by John Harkrider—a New York designer who, unlike most of his Hollywood contemporaries, was specifically credited for his work in film. Harkrider had originally been responsible for the costumes in most of Florenz Ziegfeld's Broadway shows of the 1920s, and went on to serve as a supervising art director at Universal. Two of his other 1936 films, *Three Smart Girls* and *My Man Godfrey*, had fantastic nightclub sets as well.

Swing Time's Club Raymond, again predominantly white, was decorated in a semi-nautical motif. It was inspired by both the Rainbow Room in Rockefeller Center and the Clover Club in Hollywood, a favorite gambling haunt of the movie crowd. The Club Raymond boasted a quilted ceiling and tables seating three hundred, as well as a magnificent studio-created view of New York at night. It also had a sleek cylindrical glass elevator from which guests alighted after their sixty-odd-story journey up from terra firma.

The redecorated Silver Sandal, the most stunning of the three *Swing Time* nightclubs, was saved for last. A glittering dream world of black and silver, it enhanced Fred and Ginger's "fine romance." Two huge staircases converged in a semicircle to form the club's entrance. Guests descended the staircases alongside curving tiers of tables, each table bearing a silver tablecloth and a softly glowing Saturn lamp. At the bottom of the staircases was the spacious dance floor with its design pattern of concentric diamonds in black and gray. Underneath the miraculously unsupported platform where the staircases met was the round, white bandstand, placed above a foreshortened view of midtown skyscrapers inlaid on the floor. All of this was set against huge windows revealing a star-strewn night sky, which added a shimmering undulation to Fred and Ginger's "Never Gonna Dance."

(a)

Swing Time's nightclubs: (a)   The Silver Sandal, with Georges Metaxa, Fred Astaire, Ginger
Rogers, Helen Broderick, Victor Moore.
(b, c) Club Raymond.
(d)   The redecorated Silver Sandal.

(c)

(d)

Backstage and onstage at the Paradise Night Club in *Broadway* (1929). Glenn Tryon is confronting Merna Kennedy and Evelyn Brent among the skyscraperettes on the stairs.

Working Girls (1932), with Stuart Erwin.

Winnie Lightner in *The Gold Diggers of Broadway* (1929).

Kay Francis and Lilyan Tashman polish fang and claw in the ladies' lounge from *Girls About Town* (1931).

Penthouse nightclub from *The Gold Diggers of 1935* (with Wini Shaw and Dick Powell).

In *Girl without a Room* (1932), Joyzelle performs the Dragon Dance.

Puttin' on the Ritz (1930), designed by Robert Usher.

Early Cedric Gibbons: Lew Cody and Aileen Pringle in *Adam and Evil* (1927) and a cosmetic fantasy from *Bright Lights* (1925).

John Harkrider's "Jungle Moderne" cabaret for *Three Smart Girls* (1936).

Mary Ellis and slave girls in *Paris in Spring* (1935).

Rosalie (1937).

The Last Flight (1931), with Richard Barthelmess, David Manners, Johnny Mack Brown, Walter Byron, Helen Chandler, and Elliott Nugent.

John Harkrider (below) designed this floating penthouse nightclub for Universal's *Top of the Town* (1937).

Unidentified Fox film of 1932.

William Cameron Menzies's speakeasy from *I Loved You Wednesday* (1933).

Dance Team (1932).

Transatlantic Merry-Go-Round

OCEAN LINERS

World travel reached its apex during Art Deco's heyday. Railroads were operating at a peak of efficiency and elegance, and flight, though still in its infancy, was an exciting option for those with money and daring.

For travelers voyaging between continents, there was the ultimate luxury conveyance: the ocean liner. These enormous, graceful, slightly absurd pleasure domes transcended categorization. Like their landlocked counterparts, the movie palaces, they constituted an architectural genre that was self-contained within its own world of fantasy.

But unlike movie palaces, which made no attempt to appeal to a particular class, ocean liners maintained a rigid system of social segregation. The three classes usually available were First, Cabin, and Tourist—or, more bluntly, First, Second, and Third. In most Hollywood films of the period, the latter two classes simply didn't exist. The dream aesthetic could reach new peaks in this, the most romantic and elite of all forms of travel. Why sully it with anything that smacked of the commonplace?

Ocean liners, particularly those of French origin, were the summit of contemporary decor. If their exteriors basically adhered to the practical deck-and-smoke-stack formula, their interiors were a designer's showcase. No expense was spared in obtaining the finest decorators and choicest materials. The *Île-de-France*, launched in 1926, was France's floating emissary of modern decorative art. The country's premier artists and designers were commissioned to create the ship's interior. Raymond Subes contributed the wrought iron decorations on the main staircase; Émile-Jacques Ruhlmann designed a large tearoom; Pierre Patout the main dining room (with glass decorations by René Lalique). The main salon was by Sue et Mare.

Dante's Inferno (1935), with Spencer Tracy (*right*).

For a brief time, this may well have been the world's most prestigious ocean liner. But its glory was excelled by a second French liner, the *Normandie*, only six years later.

What the *Île-de-France* was to the twenties, the *Normandie* was to the thirties. Under the terms of the contract between the French Line and the government, the *Normandie* had to "be not less than equal to the best foreign ship in commisison or under construction." The craft was greater in length than the height of the Eiffel Tower, and its gross tonnage was nearly twice that of the *Île-de-France*. With so much space in which to play, the designers (including Lalique, Jean Dunand, Jean Dupas, Raymond Subes, and Ruhlmann) had a field day. Excepting two suites in the eighteenth-century style, the entire ship was drenched in contemporary design. Author Ludwig Bemelmans, a passenger on its maiden voyage, remarked later that "she leaned to excesses in her decor—there was something of the femme fatale."

The French film industry honored the *Normandie* in 1937, when Sacha Guitry filmed the climax to his comedy *Les Perles de la couronne* in its main dining room. The largest ever on an ocean liner, this enormous space was 305 feet in length, 46 feet wide, and 25 feet high. It could seat seven hundred passengers at a time. René Lalique's dazzling lighting scheme comprised thirty-eight wall panels, two huge chandeliers, and twelve wedding-cake decorative standard lights. There were four twenty-foot-high panels of gilded plaster representing Normandy village scenes, and a twice-life-size statue in gilded bronze by Dejean. The soaring walls were encased in hammered glass, and the ceiling was a honeycomb pattern of square cove lighting.

The *Normandie* was a movie star again in Yves Mirande's *Paris–New York* (1940), starring Michel Simon and Gaby Morlay. This film featured hijinks and jewel thievery on a westward crossing, and climaxed at the 1939 New York World's Fair.

It is fortunate that Guitry and Mirande preserved the *Normandie*'s magnificence on film, for this fantasy vessel had a life span of only seven short years. In 1942, it burst into flames in New York harbor and subsequently sank during the salvage operations. Incidentally, Alfred Hitchcock used newsreel footage of the overturned *Normandie* in *Saboteur* (1942), implying that the ship's demise was a result of foul play.

Among the other Art Deco ocean liners plying the Atlantic were the *De Grasse* (1924), the *Europa* (1928), the *Lafayette* (1929), and the *Queen Mary* (1936). All would have been ideal for motion pictures, but the closest these ships came to Hollywood was New York. Hollywood chose to design its own ocean liner interiors within its studios, and exteriors could always be filmed at the harbor in nearby San Pedro.

Ocean liners were perceived by the general public as sleek symbols of the Machine Age, and Hollywood was more than willing to promote this image. They were presented as floating temples of Art Deco, often with a decidedly French design factor in keeping with the numerous French Deco ships making crossings at the time.

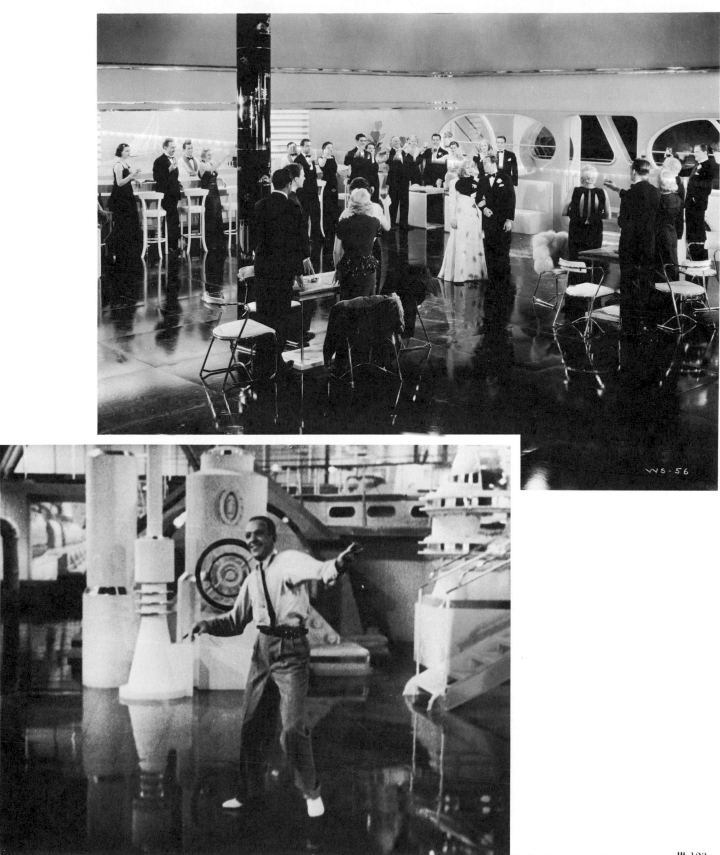

Shall We Dance (1937): Fred and Ginger in the ship's bar.
Fred Astaire dances to "Slap that Bass" in the boiler room (frame blow-up).

Typical of this sensitivity to French Deco elements was *Transatlantic* (1931), set entirely aboard a French liner. Art director Gordon Wiles showed a keen eye for modern French decor by emphasizing boldly contrasting geometric patterns and floral motifs, all of which turned up on walls, doors, screens, bedspreads, and even lampshades. The film's climax was a shoot-out between Edmund Lowe and various thugs in the bowels of the engine room. Although devoid of ornamentation, this setting carried on the Deco visual scheme by the overpowering geometry of its enormous boilers, tanks, and pistons. It anticipated the famous "Slap That Bass" number in RKO's *Shall We Dance* (1937), in which Fred Astaire danced in white deck shoes across the black Bakelite floor of an ocean liner's otherwise all-white boiler room.

The Moderne ocean liner of *Shall We Dance* was also the setting for another of the film's most appealing numbers, "Walking the Dog." Neither a song nor a dance, this was an intricately-staged silent courtship between Fred and Ginger on the promenade deck, with Gershwin's sly theme as accompaniment.

Where there were ocean liners in a Hollywood film, there was invariably romance as well. Fred and Ginger found it; so did Clark Gable and Joan Crawford in *Chained* (1934), Irene Dunne and Charles Boyer in *Love Affair* (1939), and Fred MacMurray and Carole Lombard in *The Princess Comes Across* (1936). According to Hollywood, romances born on the ocean were inevitably the springboard to a lifetime of love. The reality of the situation was usually quite different. Ocean liner historian John Malcolm Brinnin in *Beau Voyage*, remembers:

> Acquaintances struck up on crossings were inevitably fleeting. No matter how carefully shipmates might plan for eventual reunion on land, the occasion would be lost to contingency or indifference. Like an event in chemistry, shipboard friendships or romances could take place only when a particular set of conditions prevailed. To those who swore devotion to their new friends in the midships bar or the smoking room, nothing would be more unsettling than to have them turn up—obstreperous strangers at the front door—three months later.

In the landmark Deco film *Reaching for the Moon* (1931), an ocean voyage cements the relationship between Douglas Fairbanks and Bebe Daniels, which had begun on land in New York. After battling it out for six reels they finally fall in love in the seventh, and where else but on the promenade deck of *L'Amérique*. Production designer William Cameron Menzies created a ship of fantasy proportions. Scenes taking place on the promenade decks have an almost surreal quality due to their obvious soundstage locations. Rather than detracting from the film, this studio-bound quality adds to its appealing otherworldliness. The entire story appears to be unfolding on a distant Art Deco planet.

In the movies, anything could happen on an ocean liner; floating "Grand Hotel" plots insured something for everyone. Romantic intrigues were standard, but in addition there frequently were murder mystery plots blended in (*Transatlantic, The Princess Comes Across, Transatlantic Merry Go Round*) and also musical numbers (*Transatlantic Merry Go Round, Anything Goes, Reaching for the Moon*). Frank S. Nugent's *New York Times* review of *Transatlantic Merry Go Round* (1934) encapsulates the Hollywood ocean liner format film:

> A blend of "Grand Hotel" and "42nd Street," to which have been added dashes of Wheeler and Woolsey, Philo Vance and Janet Gaynor. Into what specific classification this picture should fall is more than this critic is prepared to decide. It is a drama and a melodrama, a farce and a musical comedy, a mystery story and a romance, a radio revue and a variety show—and several other things that need not be listed here. And the strange part of it all is that it manages to do fairly well in each category.

In ocean liner films, the most spectacular (and unsettling) ingredients were the storms, shipwrecks, and sinkings that often occurred as climaxes. *Whom the Gods Destroy*, a forgotten 1935 Columbia programmer, had a surprisingly large-scale shipwreck sequence. *Dante's Inferno*, also 1935, climaxed on a gambling ship with a scene in which a flambéed dessert gets out of hand and sends fire shooting up the dining-room drapes; ultimately it is the entire ship which is flambéed.[1] Perhaps the most impressive shipwreck sequence of all is in Frank Borzage's *History Is Made at Night* (1937). A liner bearing Charles Boyer and Jean Arthur is gliding through the Atlantic at night, when it suddenly crashes into an iceberg. Thousands of jagged chunks of ice thunder down onto the ship's decks, sending passengers scurrying for their lives. Such disaster scenes were thrillingly staged and, when an ocean liner epic like *Transatlantic* failed to include one, the result was an anticlimax.

As the 1930s progressed and the Streamline Moderne style took hold, the look of Hollywood's ocean liners began to change dramatically. For William Wyler's *Dodsworth* (1936) Richard Day designed an imposing all-white vessel whose spareness of ornament owed little to the French liners of just a few years before. The ocean liner in *Shall We Dance* (1937) is also white and streamlined in keeping with the RKO Astaire-Rogers style. But the ultimate Art Moderne movie liner is that of Paramount's *The Big Broadcast of 1938*. Inspired by a Norman Bel Geddes streamline original of 1932, this white teardrop-shaped ship is designed in High Movie Moderne style. Filled with broad curves, decks, and funnels, it is a perfect playground for the screwball antics of Bob Hope, Martha Raye, W. C. Fields, and Dorothy Lamour. In concept and execution, the entire boat points the way to the celebrated New York World's Fair of the following year.

[1] The *Dante's Inferno* climax was undoubtedly inspired by the decade's biggest nautical disaster. In 1933, the American cruise liner *Morro Castle* was returning from Havana when it burst into flames off the New Jersey coast near Asbury Park. One hundred thirty-four lives were lost.

The Big Broadcast of 1938: aboard the *SS Gigantic* with Dorothy Lamour and Leif Erikson. The *SS Gigantic* races the *SS Colossus* (frame blow-up).

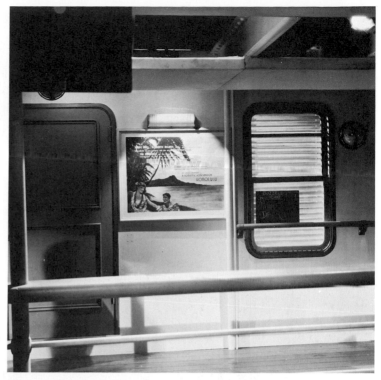

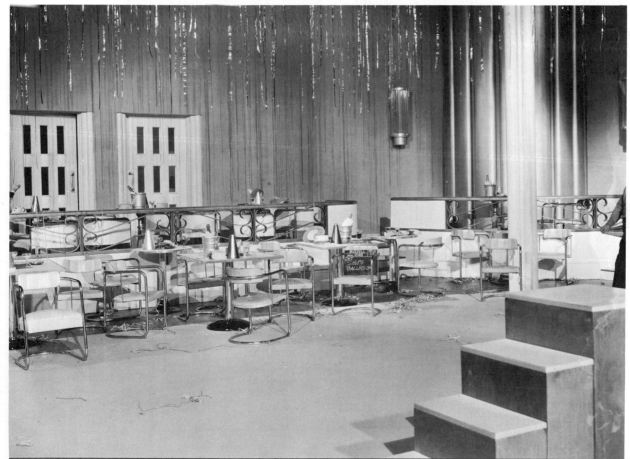

Test shots from *Honolulu* (1939).

(a)

(b)

Scenes from *Transatlantic* (1931): (a and b) Edmund Lowe and Greta Nissen.
(c) Greta Nissen with admirers Noel Madison to her left and John Halliday to her right.
(d) Tourist-class cabin.
(e) Greta Nissen and sugar daddy.

William Cameron Menzies's chimerical ocean liner in *Reaching for the Moon* (1931).

(a) Bebe Daniels.
(b) Douglas Fairbanks and Bebe Daniels.
(c) The grand staircase of *l'Amérique*.

(b)

(c)

Ship's nightclub from *Transatlantic Merry Go Round* (1934).

Ship's pool from *Transatlantic Merry Go Round*.

Gloria Swanson and Owen Moore in *What a Widow!* (1930).

Raimu and Jacqueline Delubac in *Les Perles de la couronne* (1937), filmed aboard the *Normandie*.

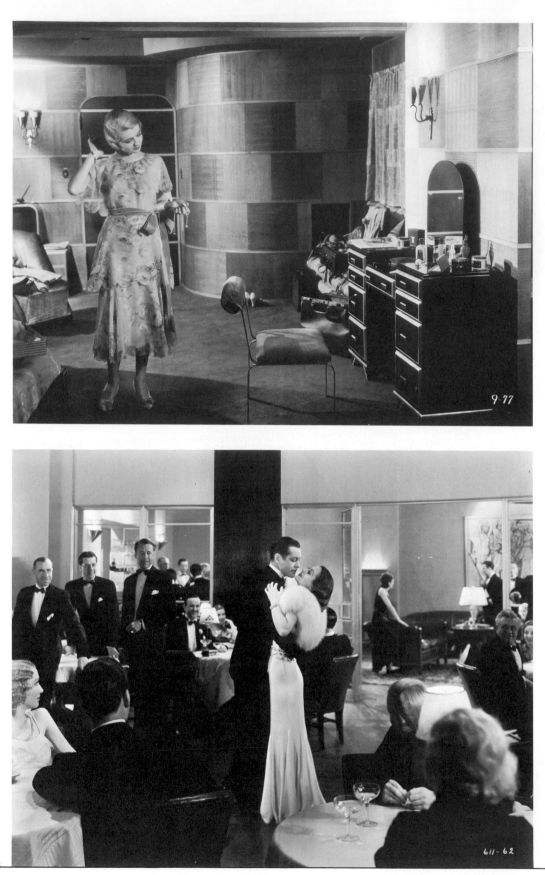

Sin Takes a Holiday (1930) with Constance Bennett.

Shipboard romance of Robert Montgomery and Joan Crawford in *Letty Lynton* (1932).

The luxury liner from *Dodsworth* (1936), designed by Richard Day.

Harpo and Chico Marx invade the ship's barber shop in *Monkey Business* (1931).

Ann Dvorak and Rudy Vallee board the ultimate Streamline Locomotive in *Sweet Music* (1935).

Go into Your Dance

MUSICALS AND EXTRAVAGANZAS

Movie musicals produced some of the most extravagant examples of the Art Deco style. They rarely faced facts, taking musical numbers beyond the parameters of the proscenium and boosting living standards in the name of glamour. As Alastair Cooke wrote of *Top Hat* (1935):

> I wish musical comedies didn't have to take quite so prosperous and Rotary a view of life. It hurts after *Alice Adams*. I for one shall enjoy watching Mr. Astaire and Miss Rogers as a mere sailor and his girl in their next film. Even then, I suppose the battleship will have a sumptuous ballroom where all the real killing is done, and I expect the port-holes serve chocolate milk-shakes at the drop of a hat.

Cooke was quite astute. Although Astaire played a gob in his subsequent picture, *Follow the Fleet* (1936), he nevertheless changed into top hat and tails to twirl Ginger around a streamlined set to the strains of "Let's Face the Music and Dance."

In his review, the perceptive Mr. Cooke anticipated yet another nautical musical of 1936, *Born to Dance.* According to an MGM publicity release, the set for the finale, "Swinging the Jinx Away," was "the world's largest musical set." This Moderne battleship of silver, glass, and alabaster, with a background of more than ten thousand stars, was sixty-five feet high and eighty-five feet wide. It provided more than enough room for the over five hundred male and female dancers, musicians, and singers.

Such opulence originated on Broadway, in the hands of a designer who never did a single movie musical. Joseph Urban, house designer for Florenz Ziegfeld, created dazzling yet tasteful stage spectacles which never eclipsed the human element: legs, breasts, thighs, and faces. Pulchritude was the outstanding commodity, and obviously one did not exhibit jewels in a pushcart. Exquisite showcases were required, as well as expressive lighting to create a three-dimensional effect.

Urban could do anything. He had gold, silver, and rhinestone fruit wired to trees; elephants spouting colored water; Venuses floating in soap bubbles; mermaids bathed in blue light; swan boats, fiestas, towering vases of roses, a miniature bridge and *bonsai* cherry trees, and a heavenly staircase surrounded by clouds.

When discovered by Ziegfeld, the Viennese-born painter, sculptor, architect, interior decorator, and scenic designer had already furnished Europe with castles, bridges, and villas. His credits included fifty theatrical productions. An exponent of the Wiener Werkstätte, Urban electrified Broadway with his lush, sophisticated decor for the *Ziegfeld Follies* and the same producer's *Midnight Frolic* (whose 1921 slogan was "See New York and Ziegfeld's girls and die").

But Urban did more than revolutionize the *Follies*—not to mention the Metropolitan Opera, where he reigned as artistic director from 1917 until his death in 1933. His scenic effects pushed decorative showmanship toward new horizons. Especially influential was his bold use of fantasy elements. Many concepts in screen musical numbers actually originated with Urban. For instance, his stage effect of feathered girls creating an illusion of oceanic foam appears in such films as *Murder at the Vanities* (1934) and *Fashions of 1934.*

Urban told *Photoplay* in 1920, "The motion picture offers incomparably the greatest field to any creative artist of brush or blueprint today. It is the art of the twentieth century and perhaps the greatest art of modern times. It is all so young, so fresh, so untried. It is like an unknown ocean stretching out before a modern Columbus." Such enthusiasm found a fruitful outlet at William Randolph Hearst's Cosmopolitan Productions. With studio facilities near the Harlem River, Urban could commute between stage and screen, glorifying Ziegfeld's girls as well as Hearst's girl, the bubbly blonde comedienne Marion Davies. Despite Hearst's meddling and the hostility of movie directors and technicians, Urban managed to devise magnificent historical re-creations for such Davies vehicles as *When Knighthood Was in Flower* (1922), a film that cost the then-incredible sum of $1,500,000. Quipped Dorothy Parker at the premiere, "Well, at least we now know what the Second Coming will be like."

The twenty-five films Urban designed for Hearst over a ten-year period often received better reviews for their decor than their dramatic content. *Photoplay* called *The Young Diana* (1922) "a style show, perhaps, but not a good motion picture. Beautiful sets, but along about the third reel, one begins to wonder if a little honest emotion wouldn't help." More effective for being less top-heavy was Urban's work for *Enchantment,* a 1921 comedy-drama with Marion Davies as the belle of Long Island's smart set. The film's sets are the first example of modern architecture in American movies. They have, wrote Randolph Carter, in *The World of Flo Zieg-*

feld, "enormous style and chic; the interiors anticipating the best of twenties design and the later Art Deco style of the thirties."

As gorgeous as the Urbanesque Art Deco sets in early talkie musicals were, their expressiveness was undermined by flat film direction. An immobile camera embalmed stage hits and vaudeville routines from the fixed perspective of a fifth-row-center orchestra seat. Enter Busby Berkeley, who understood that elaborate sets alone couldn't fascinate audiences, and that skillful camera placement and editing were absolutely essential.

Berkeley was imported to Hollywood from Broadway, where he had made a reputation for lively machinelike dance formations in twenty-one productions. (These precision routines really originated with the parade drills he devised during an army stint just after World War I.)

The musical which brought him to the West Coast was Sam Goldwyn's 1930 screen version of the Eddie Cantor smash *Whoopee.* From the start, Berkeley exploited the capabilities of the medium and made the camera an active participant in the proceedings. Whereas standard technique involved four cameras shooting from different directions, with the footage later assembled in the editing room, Berkeley used only one camera. Hal Wallis, producer of many of Berkeley's later Warners films, described Berkeley's methods: "He deliberately designed and coordinated the numbers so that when he finished shooting, it was only a matter of splicing the shots together. There was nothing left to cut, not a single frame, and no angles whatso-

A characteristically lush Joseph Urban stage set from *Ziegfeld Follies of 1927.*

ever, except those he dictated should be on screen. He literally cut his scenes in the camera." By the time Berkeley reached Warners, the entire vocabulary of film was at his command: slow pans past chorus lines, fast tracking shots for emphasis, panoramic boom shots, leggy low-angle shots, and, of course, the famed overhead shot, nicknamed "the Berkeley top-shot."

And there were the trick shots, unlike anything seen before and impossible to create in a theatre: symmetrical and geometric groupings of girls kaleidoscopically multiplied; human figures flying into the camera; jigsaw-puzzle images and bizarre angles and transitions. Such configurations were built around sets capable of opening and closing in seconds, their smooth surfaces and spacious platforms serving as playgrounds for the splendidly erotic proceedings. Berkeley was nothing if not audacious, delivering aquacades, human harps, ranks of pianos, gliding columns and mirrors, cycloramas, neon violins, mammoth rocking chairs, and endless staircases.

With the rise of Berkeley, the screen was liberated from the flowery traditions of the twenties. Dainty maidens in a mandarin's garden or the court of Versailles were usurped by Broadway Babies—a switch which had much to do with the mood of the times. Warners production head Darryl F. Zanuck, a specialist in topical subjects, sensed the need for a musical with a plot grounded in the realities of Depression America and the Broadway rat race. With numbers by Berkeley, this "New Deal in Musicals," *42nd Street* (1933), was up-to-date in every department including design.

Although Berkeley conceived the numbers, he did not design the sets. Richard Day had designed splendorous Art Deco sets for Berkeley's early Cantor vehicles at Goldwyn: notably a delightful gymnasium in *Palmy Days* (1931) and a massive girls' dormitory (with Olympic-sized pool) in *The Kid From Spain* (1932). However, it was at Warner Brothers that Berkeley's career bloomed and his greatest Art Deco set-pieces were devised. Warners had a brilliant staff of art directors to provide otherworldly environments which reflected the modernistic tastes of the period. There were Robert Haas and Willy Pogany (*Dames* [1934]), Jack Okey (*42nd Street* and *Wonder Bar* [1934]), and, perhaps most importantly, Anton Grot.

Born in Poland, Grot showed genius with perspective in his earliest film work during the 1910s. His ink and charcoal drawings not only show each set, but in addition portray lighting, camera angles, and a breakdown of the continuity of major sequences. Berkeley himself mapped out the pageantry, but he nonetheless benefited from Grot's sense of space. The settings for the musical portions of *Gold Diggers of 1933, Footlight Parade* (1933, with Okey), and *Gold Diggers of 1935* balance Berkeley's flights of fancy with starkness and economy typical of Grot. This style is in marked contrast to Cedric Gibbons's work in such MGM tuners as *Dancing Lady* (1933).

Not all of Berkeley's numbers were jazzy. He could also concoct waltz dreams like "Don't Say Goodnight" in *Wonder Bar.* In this number, the style is so hallucinogenic—a forest of silver trees, an octagon of mirrors creating reflections of dancers extending endlessly—that it might have been shot in another galaxy.

The artistry of Berkeley deserves to be taken seriously. His output has been called fascistic, sexist, decadent, and, worst of all, camp. His precise use of identically clothed and wigged multitudes has been likened to Leni Riefenstahl's Third Reich extravaganza *Triumph of the Will* (1935). He has been imitated by June Taylor and parodied by Mel Brooks. Yet no one has ever matched him. Furthermore, like Joseph Urban, he didn't strive for depersonalized spectacle. "I worked with human beings," he insisted. "It's from that you get the exhilaration. I'd always splash in a close-up to show that those lines of girls, those designs, were really human beings."

By the mid-thirties, a more performer-oriented style began to supplant the surrealism of Berkeley. Although Berkeley's numbers would open with ascending curtains and expectant audiences, once the sequence began the limitations of the proscenium arch were totally transcended. Spectacular movements of the camera elaborated block-long patterns created by chorus, props, and decor. In contrast, the intimate musicals of Fred Astaire and Ginger Rogers were structured around the romantic mobility of the two stars. As fabulous as they were, Berkeley's routines were too mammoth to enrich characters or advance the plot. In fact, all that was signified on a narrative level was that the producer of the show being mounted had a hit on his hands!

For millions of people, RKO's Astaire-Rogers series epitomizes the ideal Art Deco dreamscape, a Manhattan of the mind where nights are danced away on the gleaming floors of penthouse nightclubs, in an aura of luxury and elegance. The films feature the major motifs and materials of the Streamline Moderne period,

143

Busby Berkeley girls parading down a free-form staircase in *Gold Diggers of 1933.*

complementing the smooth sophistication of Fred and Ginger. The sets take one's breath away, but are not allowed to distract from the dances.

RKO's supervising art director Van Nest Polglase and his staff strove to create an artfully polished, self-contained world. They meticulously plotted the Moderne motifs and their coordination with every filmic element: story, choreography, costumes, even the cast's hair and skin coloring. A consistent visual strategy here was the opposition of black and white. For example, the waters of the Venetian canal in *Top Hat* (1935) were dyed black to better contrast with white marble walls. And Ginger usually had a Vaselined Latin swain to set off her blondness and whiteness.

Entire sets were emblazoned with the slender parallel lines characteristic of streamlining. Ellen Spiegel in her article for the *Velvet Light Trap*, "Fred and Ginger Meet Van Nest Polglase," itemizes streamlining of walls, floors, stairways, furniture, lamps, mirrors, and lettering found in nightclubs, private dancing clubs, ocean liners, salons, and dressing rooms. In addition, decorative schemes using geometric patterns gave plaster and chrome surfaces a real sense of depth. Within these sets, there is an interplay and contrast between the rectilinear and the curvilinear—between cylinders, spheres, and softly flowing curves, and rigorously severe angles. Spiegel notes that "round tables meet long vertical wall panels, curving double staircases have sharp-cornered steps, sinuous mouldings end in angular corners, and straight lines, whether on walls, dresses, or furniture, clash with unexpected semicircles."

Polglase's insistence on cleanly executed glossiness kept the players from seeming like wedding-cake figurines. One of his greatest creations was the make-believe Venice of *Top Hat*. Two stories high and occupying two adjoining soundstages, it boasted a winding canal spanned by three bridges, a festively decorated piazza, dance floors, balconies, and terraced cafés. This is certainly not the Venice found in guidebooks; it's the style of Radio City Music Hall—where, fittingly, most of the Astaire-Rogers confections premiered.

Others also excelled in the design of musical numbers. Merrill Pye may be buried in film history—overshadowed by Cedric Gibbons—but his creations were often rewarded by the singular credit: "Musical Presentation by Merrill Pye."

Pye began his career in the fields of architecture and furniture design, then spent most of his creative life at MGM, amassing credits spanning four decades. After pioneering screen Deco with Gibbons on *Our Modern Maidens* (1929) and *Our Blushing Brides* (1930), Pye designed such diverse films as *Freaks* (1932), *David Copperfield* (1935), and *North by Northwest* (1959). It's his musical numbers, though, that really set him apart: light yet lavish mirages for *Dancing Lady* (1933), *Reckless* (1935), *Broadway Melody of 1936* (1935), *The Great Ziegfeld* (1936), and *Born to Dance* (1936).

Corinne Griffith portrays a radiator cap ornament circa 2500 A.D. Anton Grot designed this gigantic setting for the "Mechanical Ballet" in *Lilies of the Field* (1930).

Three manifestations of the popular sunray motif: (*bottom left*) The "Pageant of the Storm" sequence from *Mlle Modiste* (1926), and musical numbers from (*top left*) *Fashions of 1934* and (*above*) *Flying High* (1931), both by Busby Berkeley.

No industrial fantasy was too far-fetched for Hollywood:
Ruby Keeler and Lee Dixon are about to tap out and type out "Too Marvelous for Words" in *Ready Willing and Able* (1937).
A vinyl-clad Alice Faye sings atop the dial of a super-duper radio in *Music is Magic* (1935).
Wall Street beauties in the finale of *Moonlight and Pretzels* (1933).

Musicals often reflected the public's mania for skyscrapers as a symbol of power and progress:
  Jack Buchanan in *Paris* (1929).
  Eleanor Powell in *Broadway Melody of 1938*.

Deco, often known as "Jazz Modern," symbolized pulsatingly up-to-date music:

Olive Borden in *The Secret Studio* (1927).

Jimmy Durante in *Hollywood Party* (1934).

Human organ pipes decorate the "I'll Sing You a Thousand Love Songs" number from *Cain and Mabel* (1936), starring Marion Davies.

Busby Berkeley girls "By
a Waterfall" (from
Footlight Parade, 1933).

Studio art directors deftly adapted concepts developed and refined by Joseph Urban.
Gold Diggers of Broadway (1929).

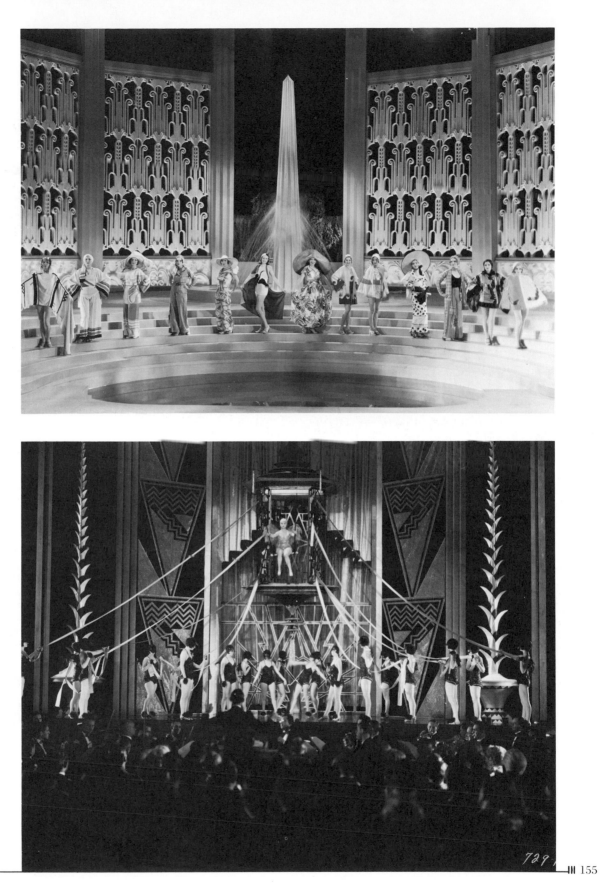

Cedric Gibbons's and Merril Pye's set for the fashion show in *Our Blushing Brides* (1930).

Louise Brooks in *The Canary Murder Case* (1929).

Man mimics machine in the "Electric Ballet," staged aboard a dirigible in Cecil B. De Mille's *Madam Satan* (1930).

Top Hat's Moderne Venice (1935).

Designer Merrill Pye used cellophane to glorify Fred Astaire and Joan Crawford in *Dancing Lady* (1933).

In this scene from *Eternally Yours* (1939), Loretta Young has just been created out of chemicals by magician David Niven.

Bottoms Up (1934).

Battleship for finale of *Born to Dance* (1936).

RKO supervising art director Van Nest Polglase.

Warner Bros. supervising art director Anton Grot.

Busby Berkeley at the center of a collage from his "Remember My Forgotten Man" finale from *Gold Diggers of 1933*.

Mary Astor in *Trapped by Television* (1936).

Just Imagine

FANTASY AND FUTURISM

Until recently, Hollywood's attitude toward period authenticity was bizarrely inconsistent. Despite superb research facilities, moviemakers wavered between reverence and revisionism. Rather than attempt the museumlike reproductions found in the British cinema, Hollywood designers usually tried to evoke the spirit of the period. MGM's Preston Ames commented in *Hollywood Speaks*:

> In motion-picture making, copy is rather a dirty word. In 1938 we did an expensive production called *Marie Antoinette* with Norma Shearer. A great many architects came to Metro to see our sets and congratulated Cedric Gibbons on his authentic reproductions of French Renaissance architecture, with particular emphasis on what he did with Versailles. Mr. Gibbons looked at these gentlemen and said, "If you will study very carefully what we did, you'll see we did everything except copy the architecture of Versailles, because if we had, photographically it would have been absolutely nothing. The moulding and design are so delicate, so sensitive, they would never have come across on the screen. So consequently, we had to redesign the entire thing so it would photograph properly!"

During the days of the studio system, slavish fidelity to period detail was thought to produce confusion and boredom in audiences; so the sort of stylization described by Preston Ames was employed, and in some cases modern touches inserted to make the far-off more familiar. For example, the court of Kublai Khan in *The Adventures of Marco Polo* (1938) was awfully Moderne for the thirteenth century. The Chinese regaled Marco Polo with their inventions, but you can be sure Bakelite was not one of them.

If such decor seems far-fetched to the eyes of today's viewers, it should be kept in mind that movies—like religious art—have always reflected the tone of the times in which they were made. Regardless of the historical period in which a film is set, contemporary styles seep in, if only in the acting. Claudette Colbert's Cleopatra behaved like the clever mistress of an out-of-town tycoon, but a more regal interpretation might not have seemed effective to 1934 audiences. Similarly, *The Adventures of Marco Polo* sets had the (non-Oriental) awesomeness which architects of Mussolini, Hitler, and American corporations strove for. The oversized marble walls spelled power to 1938 audiences, which was ultimately more important than verisimilitude.

The lightheartedness of movies like Eddie Cantor's *Roman Scandals* (1933) and *Ali Baba Goes to Town* (1937) gave designers the freedom to improvise as long as there was enough period mood to play off the star's slangy wisecracks. Laughs grew out of the spectacle of having a seriously played pageant loused up by comic bumbling. Other comedies or musicals like *The Warrior's Husband* (1933) and *The Boys from Syracuse* (1940) were also deliberately anachronistic.

Like *Cleopatra* and *The Mummy* (1932), *Roman Scandals* contains design elements which originated in an earlier civilization but were borrowed by Deco practitioners. Richard Day created a witty compromise between the ancient and the Moderne with rooms that would have looked at home on Park Avenue. A Roman beauty parlor for the "Keep Young and Beautiful" number has revolving doors between fluted columns, a glass-enclosed steam bath, and black and white slaves to provide suitable Deco contrasts.

If portraying the past gave designers freedom to embroider, then depicting the future allowed greater freedom still. Yet the future cannot be made out of whole cloth. To create the underground City of the Future, Everytown circa 2036 (in *Things to Come* [U.K., 1936]), art director Vincent Korda searched tirelessly for ideas. In his book *Charmed Lives*, Korda's son Michael recalls him "busily ransacking the libraries for avant-garde furniture designs, architectural fantasies, helicopters and autogyros, monorails and electric bubble cars, television sets and space vehicles." (The Hungarian futurist László Moholy-Nagy was also called in, but his designs were not used.) Korda and designer-director William Cameron Menzies strove to make Everytown awe-inspiring and largely succeeded despite an overpowering obstacle: H. G. Wells's unprecedented authority in adapting his novel *The Shape of Things to Come*.

Producer Alexander Korda (brother of Vincent) had given almost total control to a visionary blind to cinematic possibilities. Raymond Massey, who worked almost an entire year on the film, was appalled by Wells's screenplay: "Every trace of wit, humour and emotion, everything which made the novel so enthralling had been cut and replaced by large gobs of socialist theory." The script was revised by experienced hands like Lajos Biro, who pointed out a crucial matter in a memo to the producer: Wells had not really dreamed up an astonishing technology to characterize the future. Consequently, there is a great deal of Art Moderne in the sets: severely utilitarian furnishings in spacious, inornate rooms, using white plaster, Plexiglas, lucite, glass, and neon.

Existing modes were imaginatively revamped rather than radically reinvented. As Alastair Cooke griped:

> It must have been heartbreaking for Mr. Wells to be told that the costumes he predicted they'd be wearing in 2030 are to be the very thing in beach-wear this summer. . . . The chairs are any modern chair done in glass; they have glass elevators, but the point is—they still have elevators. By abundance of such basic details, *Things to Come* shares with most Utopias the primary error of making Today the premise, of pretending that new civilizations do not differ in kind but only in the degree of decoration, luxury, leisure, and so on.

Many of Wells's predictions did come true, but either the makers of *Things to Come* were too conservative or scientific advances too rapid. Space travel, global television, tubular glass elevators, artificial sunlight, monorail trains, and helicopters belong to this century, not the next. Michael Korda likens the set for Everytown to the Aeroport Charles-de-Gaulle outside Paris, "with its 'people-movers' conveying the crowds through glass tunnels, its indoor terraces and its chilling inhumanity." Film historian Carlos Clarens, on the other hand, compares the labyrinth to the Hyatt Embarcadero in San Francisco.

Alexander Korda was wise to engage William Cameron Menzies, the cinematic conjurer of Douglas Fairbanks's *The Thief of Bagdad* (1924). If his sets for that film seem to combine flowery early French Deco motifs with the style of 1920s storybooks, it might be noted that Menzies, like Joseph Urban, started his career illustrating children's books. He later became the most respected and highest paid designer of his generation, receiving in 1929 the first Academy Award ever given for art direction, for *The Tempest* and *The Dove* (both 1928 productions). Although as director of *Things to Come* he was unable to breathe life into the characters, his dynamically balanced compositions kept the eyes of audiences alert during the most long-winded of speeches. Menzies's own eyes were once flatteringly compared to a two-inch lens. His whole approach, in fact, embodied an unceasing awareness of the camera eye, with sets built to show only what the camera would see.

The exact extent of Menzies's design contribution to *Things to Come* is difficult to determine, and not only because of the presence of Vincent Korda and special effects wizard Ned Mann, who handled the miniature work. The shadow of H. G. Wells crept into every corner of the film. Menzies had every right to consider the author a "very testy man," inundated as he was by Wells's high-handed criticisms. He received thumbnail sketches mapping out the blocking of the actors, and memos suggesting design improvements. Sample: "This is all wrong. Get it in better perspective. The film is an H. G. WELLS film and your highest best is needed for the complete realization of my treatment. Bless you." Nevertheless, in their profile of Menzies in *fantascene 4* magazine, Scott Holton and Robert Skotak see him as the true author of the film:

> While the specific designing tasks had been relegated to others (settings by Vincent Korda; costumes by John Armstrong, René Hubert and the Marchioness of Queensbury, etc.) the overall production design concepts were those of Menzies. In the final analysis it was his contribution that lent dignity and prestige to the great author's untypically labored screenplay.

Wells denounced Fritz Lang's *Metropolis* (Germany, 1927) for scientific speciousness. Its climax must have been especially offensive to Wells's technocratic sensibilities: the ultimate victory of human emotions over machines. The brilliance of the film's direction and design was apparently lost on Wells.

Lang, trained as an architect, maintained remarkable formal control over the film, manipulating shots and geometric forms within shots with a keen understanding of their psychological effect on audiences. *Metropolis* is dominated by cubistic architecture and the geometric patterns created by painted shadows and surging crowds. For example, the bodies of children form a pyramid around the heroine during a devastating flood. Movement is stylized—as in the rhythmic pounding of the feet of slave workers through underground corridors and the manipulation of the hands on gigantic dials with exaggeratedly jerky gestures. Such Expressionistic devices make the equation of people with machines solemnly explicit.

The art directors Otto Hunte, Erich Kellethut, and Karl Vollbrecht surrealistically rendered skyscrapers joined by hanging streets and freeway bridges, but their architecture for the year 2000 was rooted in the 1920s.

Lang's 1924 trip to New York actually served as the film's inspiration. From the deck of the *Deutschland,* he

> . . . saw a street lit as if in full daylight by neon lights and topping them oversized luminous advertisements moving, turning, flashing on and off, spiraling . . . something which was completely new and nearly fairy-tale-like for a European in those days, and this impression gave me the first thought of an idea for a town of the future. . . . The buildings seemed to be a vertical veil, shimmering, almost weightless, a luxurious cloth hung from the dark sky to dazzle, distract and hypnotize. At night the city did not give the impression of being alive; it lived as illusions lived. I knew then that I had to make a film about all these sensations.

If Germany's *Metropolis* had lofty aims, its American counterpart *Just Imagine* (1930) aimed only to prove that boy will still get girl in 1980, even if he's addressed as J-21 and she's LN-18. The colossal Deco "Gotham" designed by Stephen Gooson and Ralph Hammeras helped sell this science fiction musical conceived and scored

Semihistorical throne rooms: *Cleopatra* (1934) and . . .

The Adventures of Marco Polo (1938).

The Warrior's Husband (1933).

by the team of DeSylva, Brown, and Henderson. Ads raved about "New York gone futuristic . . . a towering tangle of pinnacles, viaducts, bridges . . . and what fashions in dress." And if publicity releases are to be trusted, its major miniature (although not referred to as such) was said to have taken 205 engineers and craftsmen five months to build at a cost of $168,000.

This sum was many times what Universal spent on its chapter serials *Flash Gordon* and *Buck Rogers*, each of which exposed its comic strip hero, played by Buster Crabbe, to the perils of a low-budget future. No attempt was made to explain how Roman-style helmets could co-exist with disintegrating-ray guns. It was all pure fantasy, cheerfully amalgamating thirties styles with Oriental, Ottoman, medieval, operetta, and what have you.

Other fantasy films, dealing with neither the past nor the future, also adapted modern architecture to suit their needs. Horror stories and fables about mythical kingdoms reflected new trends in design, modifying, magnifying, or distorting to create precise moods.

Universal's *The Black Cat* (1934) was the most overtly Bauhaus film ever made by an American studio. Directed by German emigré Edgar G. Ulmer, this horror classic (having absolutely nothing to do with Edgar Allan Poe) used modern architecture as a background for a particularly perverse brand of evil. Ulmer had begun his career as a set designer for Max Reinhardt in Germany, and subsequently became assistant art director on all of F. W. Murnau's American films. A Germanic influence permeated *The Black Cat*, and it is reasonable to assume that Ulmer had as much to do with the Bauhaus-Expressionistic decor as art director Charles D. Hall.

Boris Karloff starred as Poelzig (named after the German Expressionist designer Hans Poelzig), a devil-worshipper and necrophile who has built a modern mansion over a battlefield. The house is a cold and glossy marvel of glass brick, Bakelite floors, and curving metal staircases. Furnishings include glass tables, Breuer chairs, and digital clocks. "When one sees *The Black Cat* today," mused Ulmer in an interview, "one realizes that the set could have been conceived by Poelzig twenty years after the film was made." The set was also a model of economy, budgeted at only $3,700.

If the style of *The Black Cat* is inclined to produce the jitters, then the symmetry of *Lost Horizon*'s (1937) Shangri-La is surely meant to produce the opposite effect. Stephen Gooson's majestic lamasery evokes heaven in the Himalayas: a place of peace and contentment overlooking the mythical valley of the Blue Moon. Constructed on the Columbia ranch, the structure was ninety feet tall and took 150 men two months to complete. No expense was spared by the usually penny-pinching Columbia Pictures.

However, the Utopian vision of director Frank Capra and designer Stephen Gooson remains controversial to this day. Critic Elliott Stein mentions Shangri-La's "vast ghastliness." John Baxter, on the other hand, asserts in *Fantasy Films* that "the film's design is quietly balanced and restrained; white walls, pools that mirror overhanging trees, graceful walks and gardens combine the best of thirties architecture with an Oriental serenity." Graham Greene, writing at the time of the picture's release, definitely would have preferred more asceticism. "This Utopia closely resembles a film star's luxurious estate in Beverly Hills: flirtatious pursuits through grape arbors, splashings and divings in blossomy pools under improbable waterfalls, and rich and enormous meals."

Not all hidden civilizations are as benign as Shangri-La. H. Rider Haggard's *She,* filmed by RKO in 1935, features a predatory queen fated to live forever. Long considered a lost film, it was revived during Radio City Music Hall's 1976 Art Deco Week, and during its Los Angeles engagement the following year, the *Los Angeles Times* complimented its "monumental sets designed in a kind of Art Deco Barbaric."

Designers of the 1939 San Francisco Golden Gate Exposition may have been influenced by the *Lost Horizon* sets. More likely, both extravaganzas drew upon the same Pacific architectural styles, and the ostentatious neoclassicism of fascist Germany and Italy. Similarly, the resemblance between the 1939 New York World's Fair and the Utopian Emerald City of *The Wizard of Oz* (1939) cannot be considered purely coincidental.

Of course, it's not surprising that such resemblances exist. World's fairs and movie sets are actually close relatives: both well-planned fantasies designed for a limited run. The impermanence of these structures allows for lighter building materials and a lighter overall tone. There's no need for the inhibiting dignity that comes with delusions of immortality.

In constructing an actual office or apartment building, comfort and efficiency are key considerations. But designers of world's fairs and movies can relax such practical restrictions. For example, the sets for *Our Dancing Daughters* were far too sleek for habitation, and included such features as a staircase going nowhere. Similar architectural experimentation and playfulness suffuse world's fair design. Established styles are elaborated or simplified, and future styles previewed.[1]

[1] A number of thirties films featured fairs without actually taking the leading players on location. A small section of the fair would be re-created on a soundstage, and stock footage, back projection, or doubles would do the rest. *Hoopla* climaxed with Clara Bow's dance inflaming the 1933 Chicago World's Fair, and there were some sketchy shots of the 1939 San Francisco World's Fair in *Charlie Chan at Treasure Island,* but not surprisingly it was the 1939 New York fair which got the most coverage. In *Remember?* (1939) Robert Taylor and Greer Garson rode the tractor train across a process screen of Constitution Mall. In *Mr. and Mrs. Smith* (1941) Carole Lombard and Gene Raymond found themselves stuck atop the parachute-jump tower. Most panoramic of all was *Eternally Yours* (1939), with David Niven parachuting over Flushing Meadow as Loretta Young waited below in a studio mockup of the fair's amusement area. Even animators Max and Dave Fleischer got into the act with *All's Fair at the Fair* (1939), in which two country bumpkins gawked at the World of Tomorrow.

From *She* (1935), "Ceremony of the Flame"——the yearly ritual of the lighting of the sacred fires, with Helen Mack as fuel.

Eddie Cantor and Doris Davenport tour a fantasy ice-cream factory in the Technicolor finale to *Kid Millions* (1934).

The robot Maria (Brigitte Helm) performs a shimmy in *Metropolis* (1927).

Groucho Marx holds court in the streamlined mythical kingdom of Fredonia in *Duck Soup* (1933).

(a)

(b)

The sky's the limit: vehicular traffic as envisioned by Hollywood. (a) Jimmy Durante and Polly Moran in *Hollywood Party* (1934); (b) Charles Farrell in *Liliom* (1930); (c) Alexander Gray and Bernice Claire in *No No Nanette* (1930).

(c)

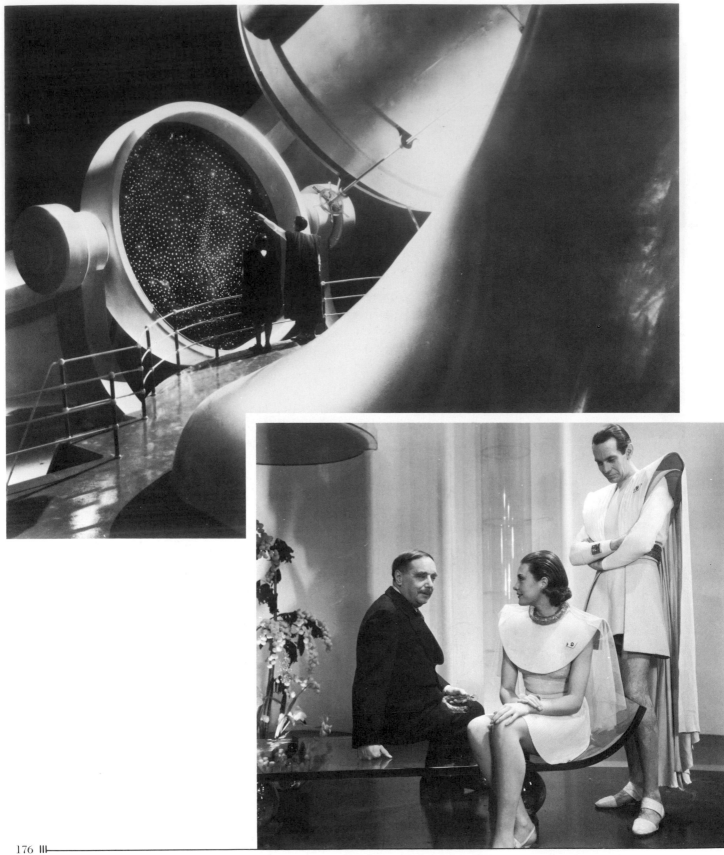

H. G. Wells, seen chatting with *Things to Come* (1936) cast members Pearl Argyle and Raymond Massey (All photos on pages 176, 177, and 178 are from *Things to Come*).

Art director William Cameron Menzies.

Things to Come.

Evil is allied with modern architecture in *The Black Cat* (1934), with Boris Karloff, Bela Lugosi, and Lucille Lund.

The controversial lamasery of *Lost Horizon* (1937).

New York 1980 as seen in the musical fantasy *Just Imagine* (1930).

Aboard the zeppelin of Cecil B. De Mille's *Madam Satan* (1930).

Medicine marches on: El Brendel's operation from *Just Imagine* (1930).

A fantasy butcher shop: Munsinger's Modern Market, in *Five and Ten* (1931).

The skyline of *Metropolis* (1927).

The streamlined observatory for the Ritz Brothers' "He Ain't Got Rhythm" number from *On the Avenue* (1937).

The Trylon and Perisphere, symbols of the 1939 New York World's Fair.

The Perisphere and Paul Manship's giant sundial on Constitution Mall at the New York World's Fair of 1939.

Pick a Star

PORTRAITS

Art Deco stars? Stars were flesh and blood, not chrome and Bakelite. However, certain performers, by virtue of their poise and physique, exemplified Art Deco's conception of the human form. Such qualities were enhanced in studio portraits by the use of modernistic props and settings as well as stylized lighting.

If female stars tend to dominate this selection, it is because the female form was itself a key element of the Art Deco style. Clocks, porcelain figurines, table lamps, art, and sculpture all depicted willowy sprites in highly idealized poses. In addition, melodramas and sophisticated comedies (the film genres which most often utilized Art Deco settings) almost always had female stars as their focal points.

Surely the grace of such stars as Norma Shearer and Fred Astaire helped inspire the sumptuous settings seen in these pages.

Laura La Plante

Dolores Del Rio

Jean Harlow

Gloria Swanson

Tallulah Bankhead

P1246-45

Louise Brooks

DWS. 84

Pauline Starke

Alice Faye

Gail Patrick

Kay Francis

Constance Bennett

Nancy Carroll

Helen Kane

Bebe Daniels

Brigitte Helm

Evelyn Brent

Eleanor Powell

Joan Crawford

Carole Lombard

Myrna Loy

Fay Wray

Alice White

Franchot Tone

Chester Morris

Cary Grant

Warner Baxter

Warren William

Robert Montgomery

William Haines

Douglas Fairbanks, Jr.

Adolphe Menjou

Ginger Rogers

Fred Astaire

Index

ERIC MYERS is a New York-based motion picture publicist and writer. His articles on film have appeared in *International Photographer, Diversion, Variety, Marquee,* and *Cinema Journal.* He has handled publicity for the films *Sophie's Choice, The World According to Garp, Trading Places,* and many others. He holds degrees in cinema studies from UCLA and the University of Paris.

HOWARD MANDELBAUM has built a career on film history and exhibition. From 1971 to 1977 he managed a film society devoted to the rediscovery of neglected American movies. He has planned film programs and written notes for Queens College, the University of Connecticut, Carnegie Hall Cinema and the Thalia Theater, both in New York, and the Museum of Modern Art. He is co-founder of Phototeque, a research library for motion picture production stills, and co-author of the popular Hollywood gossip compendium *Flesh and Fantasy.*